Violence and Islam

ADONIS

Violence and Islam

Conversations with Houria Abdelouahed

Translated by David Watson

polity

First published in French as *Violence et Islam. Entretiens avec Houria Abdelouahed*, ©
Éditions du Seuil, 2015

This English edition © Polity Press, 2016

Polity Press
65 Bridge Street
Cambridge CB2 1UR, UK

Polity Press
350 Main Street
Malden, MA 02148, USA

ISBN-13: 978-1-5095-1190-7

A catalogue record for this book is available from the British Library.

Library of Congress Cataloging-in-Publication Data
Names: Adonis, 1930- interviewee. | Abdelouahed, Houriya, interviewer.
Title: Violence and Islam : conversations with Houria Abdelouahed / Adonis.
Other titles: Violence et Islam. English
Description: English edition. | Malden, MA : Polity, 2016. | Includes
    bibliographical references.
Identifiers: LCCN 2016023813 (print) | LCCN 2016030363 (ebook) | ISBN
    9781509511907 (hardcover : alk. paper) | ISBN 1509511903 (hardcover : alk.
    paper) | ISBN 9781509511921 (mobi) | ISBN 9781509511938 (epub)
Subjects: LCSH: Violence--Religious aspects--Islam. | Violence in the Qur?an.
    | Ad?un?is, 1930---Interviews.
Classification: LCC BP190.5.V56 A35513 2016 (print) | LCC BP190.5.V56 (ebook)
    | DDC 297.2/7--dc23
LC record available at https://lccn.loc.gov/2016023813

Typeset in 11pt on 15pt Minion Pro by Servis Filmsetting Ltd, Stockport, Cheshire
Printed and bound by CPI Group (UK) Ltd, Croydon

The publisher has used its best endeavours to ensure that the URLs for external websites
referred to in this book are correct and active at the time of going to press. However,
the publisher has no responsibility for the websites and can make no guarantee that a
site will remain live or that the content is or will remain appropriate.

Every effort has been made to trace all copyright holders, but if any have been
inadvertently overlooked the publisher will be pleased to include any necessary credits
in any subsequent reprint or edition.

For further information on Polity, visit our website: politybooks.com

Contents

Preface

The death of the Prophet Muhammad was followed by the founding of the first caliphate and the transformation of Islam into a political regime. Religion itself was used in power struggles. The people, who were 'one' around the Prophet, experienced division, discord and war. Islam thus became an ideological war, and the Qur'an was interpreted according to these conflicts of interest. This is how the culture of *ḥadīth* and *al-ijmā'* (consensus) came into existence.

The Islam of today is this historical Islam.

This book of dialogues deals with this Islam and the culture that derives from it. To avoid any confusion, it is purely about this political Islam that has existed since the first caliphate to the present day.

We hope to discuss violence in Islam from a philosophical and psychoanalytical point of view in another work.

Adonis and Houria Abdelouahed
Paris, August 2015

vii

A Spring Without Swallows

H: Adonis, how do we explain the failure of the Arab Spring?

A: In the beginning, the Arab uprising brought to mind an awakening. A very beautiful awakening. But the events that have followed in the wake of this Arab Spring have demonstrated that it wasn't a revolution, but rather a war, one which, instead of opposing tyranny, has itself become another form of tyranny. Of course, there were forces of opposition that didn't have recourse to violence. But these were crushed beneath the weight of the events that followed the beginning of the uprising. Moreover, this revolution has shown that it is confessional, tribal and not civil, Muslim and not Arab. Yet the situation of Arab society needed to change radically.

H: By 'radically' I assume you mean in political, social, economic and cultural terms.

A: Exactly. The problem is that this change came up against the eternal questions of religion and power. The people, who had had their rights abused, dreamed only of overthrowing the existing forms of power without paying sufficient attention to the question of institutions, education, family, the freedom of women and of the individual. So there was a lack of reflection on the way of founding a civil society, namely the society of the citizen.

H: So we might say that individuals, oppressed as they were by political power, did not work towards a genuine change and were unable to think about the complexity inherent in all change.

A: Absolutely. It was to do with an error of vision: it is impossible in a society like Arab society to create a revolution unless it is based on secular principles. Moreover, the organic relationship between the rebels who claimed to adhere to this so-called revolution and foreign forces was a second mistake. Instead of thinking of themselves as independent, the rebels aligned themselves closely with foreign forces.

H: Was it these individuals who sought the West's intervention or was it the West that took advantage of the situation to gain purchase on the start of a revolt?

A: Both. And the consequences have been disastrous. The alliance with foreigners has compromised the movement. I might add that the armed violence has played a large role in the destruction of the revolution. Sophisticated weapons flooded in from outside. We know that the revolutionaries could only have acquired these arms from foreign forces. As a result, instead of destabilizing the dictatorial regimes, they have destroyed their countries.

H: But if we take the example of Syria, the regime has also wreaked a terrible carnage and played its role in the destruction.

A: That's true. But a revolution that seeks change cannot destroy its own country. It's true that the regime was violent, but the rebels should have avoided dragging the country into chaos. To cap it all, fundamentalism is back, better organized and more cruel. From hope and a desire to see better days, we have sunk into obscurantism. Instead of change full of hope, we are living through a genuine disaster. Further, not a word has been uttered about the freedom of women. Can we talk about an Arab revolution if women are still prisoners of Sharia Law? Recourse to religion has transformed this spring into a living hell. Religion has been interpreted and used for ideological ends.

H: Is the problem that the religious types have taken advantage of the unstable situation to reverse the revolution, or is it that the Arab Muslim remains, deep down, fundamentally religious?

A: A revolution is supposed to reflect the level of the revolutionaries. So the importance of a revolution in a given country comes from the quality of the revolutionaries, from their culture, from their relationship to secular values, from their vision of the world and worldly things. What has happened in the name of the revolution in the Arab countries proves that the large majority of Arab society is still dominated by ignorance, illiteracy and religious obscurantism. A revolution that descends into obscurantism has nothing to do with true revolution. It's a catastrophe, because we set out towards a future full of promise but today we are in retreat. It's a complete regression.

H: And in this regression we encounter something familiar, something well known. In *Al-Kitāb III*, you say: 'Aleppo – How many times you have revolted. The sword sliced off the heads of your rebel sons . . . / How many times you have embraced tyrants!' When we read these verses, it as if we are reading about the Aleppo of today. In your view, what is the meaning of this repetition? Why, after fifteen centuries, are we still subjected to the Law of the Sword?

A: There has been a lot of talk about the Arab Spring as if it had nothing to do with the past. Yet it is clearly related to our history. Firstly, people seem to forget that we have known revolutions which have been more radical than that promised by the Arab Spring. That of the Zinj,[1] for example, known as the 'Revolt of the Blacks'. Then there was the revolution of the Qarmatians,[2] who called for the establishment of a system that today we would label socialist. That is not to mention other, smaller revolutions that called for liberty and equal rights. These revolutions, both large and small, were more important and more radical than the Arab Spring.

H: I have something to add here: I never heard tell of either the Zinj revolution or the Qarmatian revolution during my primary or secondary education in Morocco. Our school books kept us in complete ignorance. It was during my university studies in France that I discovered these protest movements and heard about their extraordinary struggles against power and against racial and social discrimination.

A: The problem is that our history remains the history of a dictatorial regime and not that of the people, just as our culture is the culture of power and of the reigning regime. There is no mention of the people, nor of its revolts, and even less of its aspirations. The emphasis is constantly on the caliphate of God; the rights of citizens are completely overlooked.

H: It's true that in order to know about these sequences of Arab history you have to have an immense curiosity and a taste for subversive literature. The *firaq bāṭinīya* (Batinite groups[3] who had a political vision, such as the Qarmatians) are not taught in schools. And as there are secret police roaming university campuses, their name is not even mentioned.

A: The Qarmatians represented an appeal for equality, the sharing of wealth and a fight against misery and poverty. They were progressive and extolled socialist values. In their vision, the individual works and contributes to the enrichment of the public treasury, which in turn redistributes money to the people, according to each individual's need and the work he or she does.

H: They were pioneers of Marxism. Theirs was a revolt against the spirit of ʿUthmān, the third caliph, who was Muhammad's son-in-law, and who excessively enriched his family and the future Umayyads.

A: You could say that they rose up against the practices of the first Islam, that of the caliphate.

H: 'Uthmān, who was twice Muhammad's son-in-law, forgot about the people as soon as he became caliph. God's representative on earth became the most unjust of men.

A: That is why he was besieged, and later assassinated, at Medina in 656 (AD). The revolution against 'Uthmān gathered together insurgents from Mecca, Kufa (in Iraq) and Egypt. This revolution represented a high-water mark of political consciousness and a major protest movement.

H: As for the Zinj, that is, the Blacks, they fought against racism and social discrimination.

A: The Zinj opposed servitude. They called for the abolition of social discrimination based on the difference between 'races'. Proclaiming justice for all, they defended the idea of citizenship and equal rights. Citizenship should be based on something more than skin colour or social class. It was this desire that animated their revolt. They were more radical and more advanced than the rebels of the Arab Spring.

H: But they were opposed and exterminated. These exterminations are part of the history of Islam. This is the lesson of the historical sources on which *Al-Kitāb* is based.

A: When we speak of Islam in this context, we have to distinguish two levels: the theoretical level closely bound up with power, and the constitutional and practical level.

The first level stays unchanged. We can summarize it in the following way: Islam is based on three essential points. Firstly, Muhammad is the Prophet of Prophets. Secondly, the truths he transmits are consequently ultimate truths. Thirdly, the individual or the believer can add or change nothing; they have to content themselves with obeying the precepts. Throughout history power has demonstrably overseen this unchanging perpetuation of the concept of religion which I have just outlined.

H: Like a snake eating its own tail: the king derives authority from heaven and heaven is defended by a king who applies the precepts of heaven.

A: Have we thought long and hard enough about that expression: 'The caliph is the representative of God'? You can't be the representative of God, it's contrary to the very notion of the divine. Let us recall that the Prophet designated himself as 'the servant of God and His messenger'.

H: The king is the representative on earth . . .

A: Logically, man cannot represent God. The caliph can represent the Prophet. The Prophet, like all men, can commit errors. Calling the caliph the representative of God is tantamount to saying that he is God on earth.

H: To the extent that the caliph can pass himself off as infallible. Perhaps that is one explanation of the lack of revolt. To be discontent with the caliph or the monarch ultimately means to be discontent with God.

A: Anyone who opposes this representative of God is considered a renegade. Moreover, Islam fought against the civilizations that preceded it. And it drew a black-and-white picture of the world devoid of any plurality. Its motto was: no design, no law, no plan can equal the vision of the representative of God. This comes down to saying: don't dream of a better future but submit to, and apply the letter of, this orthodox and dogmatic vision of the world that has predominated since the beginning of Islam.

H: We might say that the past remains an ideal that cannot be dethroned or surpassed. Knowing only how to live in the embrace of the past, individual Arabs lack the wherewithal to make a revolution.

A: Any future lies in the past. That's where the repetition comes from. The remains of the past are constantly recycled. The present is confused with the past. Having said that, let us not forget that there have always been innovators in every field in the Arab and Muslim world. Nevertheless, these innovators have never espoused religious dogma as it is practised by the caliphs or the monarchs.

H: But you also say that the great innovators have always been attacked by the political powers-that-be.

A: Indeed. But in truth all the creators, all those who have written works in the fields of poetry, philosophy, music, etc., those who built Islamic culture or Arab civilization, were not Muslims in the traditional sense of the word. For example, the great poets such as Abū Nuwās,[4] al-Mutanabbī,[5] al-Ma'arrī,[6] etc., were against the official religion. And no philosopher has ever been, strictly speaking, a believer or a religious person. Those who created Islamic civilization transgressed Islam in the dogmatic sense of the word. All this needs rethinking.

H: We have a duty to rethink the fundamentals of our religion: women, slavery, adoption, filiation, etc., and everything that constitutes civility and the construction of society. A revolution that culminates in the birth of Daesh and its catalogue of cruelty demands and requires that we rethink our history.

A: In the light of all that, we can say that this Arab Spring has nothing whatever to do with revolution or with the liberation of peoples. It is tainted with obscurantism just like any dictatorial regime. It is more terrible and more bloody than all the dictatorial regimes in the Arab world. Daesh and Al-Nusra, to name but these two groups, are just as cruel, if not more so. Moreover, the Arab regimes have shown that they were no more than puppets in the hands of foreign forces, insignificant, unwitting puppets in a strategy and a game that are beyond their ken. There is an economic and strategic conflict between, on the one hand, the Americans and Europeans and, on the other, China, Russia and other countries.

H: The eternal economic and political interests.

A: That's it. We should recall that most of the political speeches and decisions attest that Saudi Arabia and Qatar were the first to have financed and armed the opposition to the Syrian regime. So that leads us to the following conclusion: that this is more about economic and strategic interests than revolution.

H: It all began with Mohamed Bouazizi setting himself alight – after he had been humiliated – and culminated in the engagement of Arabs in a war machine.

A: As if the primary motivation had not been the overthrow of regimes to institute democracy and liberate the people, but economic enrichment and strategic control. All the regimes that put up any sort of resistance were destroyed. The Saudis and the Qataris undeniably played a part in this disaster that the Arab world is going through right now.

H: There is talk also of redrawing the map of the Arab world. It began with Iraq, then Libya, then Syria and the war against Yemen . . .

A: Indeed, there is undeniably a strategic aspect to this, a plan to redraw the near East. This is not unconnected to the schism in the heart of Islam between Sunnis and Shias and the old conflict around the caliphate or the exercise of power. This conflict is exploited by the Western powers, who direct the regimes to suit their own interests.

H: It's highly complex, as all these aspects – strategic, political and religious – are entangled. But I feel that we are forgetting the psychological aspect. Mesopotamia is still the cradle of civilization. Not just the human is being destroyed, but also the remains of a pre-Islamic era. These traces are being wiped out, and this action responds to the most instinctive of drives: the drive to destruction.

A: Absolutely. This region of the world is under attack strategically and culturally. Its destruction is under way. The result of the Arab Spring is a complete failure.

The Necessity
of Rereading:
History and Identity

H: 'The historian's task is to offer a "true" narrative in order to give the "best possible" representation of the past, one that is separated from the present and which, in principle, implies the belief that there are discontinuities and differences between times.'[1] How is it that in the Arab world, even today, there is a glaring lack of any historical study in the modern sense of the term, that our touchstones remain Tabarī[2] and Ibn Kathīr,[3] authors from the early centuries of the Hijra, who confuse history and legend? Why can't we blow away the cobwebs and produce some more modern readings of history?

A: Even from a poetic point of view, the Arabs haven't, for example, written a single book on the aesthetics of Arabic and its specificity. We might put this down to a lack of a spirit of research and innovation. It is as if the Arabs of today have no questioning spirit. In terms of history, the Arabs can't seem to think objectively about the first so-called Arab-Muslim state, which was founded on the power and cohesion of the tribe. The word tribe implies an absence of the idea of plurality. The Quraysh, the tribe of Muhammad which held power in the caliphate after the Prophet's death, was a single family that founded a state based on Saqīfa.[4] Even the Anṣār, who defended Muhammad against his Quraysh enemies, were excluded from the exercise of power at the point of a sword. The Anṣār proposed a form of coalition. Sa'd ibn 'Ubāda al Anṣārī asked for a share of power; in other words, for a form of democracy allowing them to participate in political life alongside the Quraysh. But 'Umar and the Quraysh refused to share power. Sa'd was attacked and chased out of Saqīfa along with other Anṣār. Power was in the hands of the tribe. Since then, history has been closely connected to the power of the tribe.

H: But why has writing on history not been brought up to date? Why, despite a renaissance in the Arab world from the end of the nineteenth century to the beginning of the twentieth, have intellectuals failed to produce modern readings of ancient texts?

A: When I wrote *Ath-thābit wa'l mutahawwil* (*The Static and the Dynamic*),[5] academics criticized me for reading or rereading history differently. In an attempt to restrict interest in my work they accused me of being a Shi'ite who was distorting the history of the Arabs. In other words, my reading wasn't the product of personal reflection, deep thinking and research, and a genuine desire to move beyond traditional, impoverished and repetitive readings, but rather motivated solely by my 'hostility towards the Sunni'. In this work I talked about the Sunni state and revolutions against this state over the course of history. But those academics who criticized me didn't propose any alternative studies to discuss my theses or points of view. They attacked my place of birth. This is the voice of the tribe, not that of an objective researcher.

H: It was as if your study were based on a purely ideological position. Did you defend yourself?

A: I didn't defend myself, even though, deep down, I was very unhappy that my work had been so badly read and interpreted. But over time the reading of this book evolved. People became less reticent.

H: It was even translated into Indonesian and superbly received. Your experience with *Ath-thābit wa'l mutaḥawwil* reminds me of that of Taha Hussein and his book *Fī ash-shi'r al-jāhilī* (*On Pre-Islamic Poetry*). Taha Hussein was condemned and forced to rewrite his work, simply because he tried to rethink pre-Islamic poetry with reference to the *cogito*, even though it contained no critique of religion and cast no doubt on Qur'anic verses.

A: It is unfortunately the case that Arab thinking, even that which has been labelled modern, remains dogmatic and trapped within the tribal mentality. Nothing is to be changed, nothing shaken up. Everything must stay exactly the same as before, set in stone. What we have called *'aṣr an-nahḍa* (the Arab renaissance) turns out to have been a false renaissance. But we can't reread history or analyse it or move it forwards if we don't free ourselves of this tribal mentality.

H: What happened to Taha Hussein makes one thing clear to us. Basically, it is the critical spirit itself that is condemned, not its questioning of pre-Islamic verses.

A: The 'Islamic regime' was born as a political and economic power. Without the tribal mentality it would not have enjoyed the success that it has. Drawing, among other things, on the force of the tribal mentality, Islam very quickly became a means of power and conquest.

H: By 'very quickly' and 'from the start' I assume you mean 'since the death of the Prophet'?

A: Yes. Since the death of Muhammad. As I said earlier, the drama all started at Saqīfa. In fact, Saqīfa has never ceased to be a presence in the Arab space. It inhabits this space. We remain enshrouded in Saqīfa. For fifteen centuries, the Arab–Arab war has been waged incessantly. This problem is still with us today. We haven't left the Middle Ages yet.

H: In his *L'Identité nationale, une énigme*, Marcel Detienne writes: 'to be born of your own place, to be the product of it, and why not?, to be agent of your own history'. I get the feeling that something in our history is preventing us from being agents of our own history.

A: We have discussed the shackles of religion. Since Islam was born perfect, it stands against everything that came before and everything that has followed since. That 'everything' includes philosophy, art, thought, creativity, a vision of the world, etc. With thinking abolished and art condemned, the only illumination we have is that offered by the reigning power. The drama of Saqīfa is still playing out today. Why is Saudi Arabia conducting a war in Yemen? The roots of this war lie deep in the tribal spirit of our history. But instead of analysing the reasons for this havoc, we are supposed to just carry on repeating these wars without ever questioning the basis of them. In the traditionalist mindset, you have to be a 'follower' (*tābi'*) and not a 'questioner'. We have to simply repeat and reproduce.

H: And reproduce identically.

A: Identically, because perfection has already been attained. The past embraces this perfection, which to this day remains the only model, the only example to follow. We are called upon to remain in complete concordance and agreement with the past. Thus identity is reduced to sheer repetition. If you want to be a Muslim, or rather an Arab-Muslim, you have to imitate the perfection of history.

H: In psychoanalysis we call this state of things 'a frozen time'. It is the frozen time of a suffering psyche. However, Daesh merely repeats the dark side of history. Daesh does not repeat the genius of an Averroes,[6] an Alhazen[7] or an Ibn 'Arabī,[8] or the bold speculative thinking of the Mu'tazilites.[9]

A: Daesh repeats what is connected to power, not thought or research. That's another reason why we are still in Saqīfa, why the spirit of Saqīfa still reigns and dominates everyday life today. So identity, in this way of seeing things, remains a repetition. It's a heritage, not something that has been freely chosen. Individuals are born Arab-Muslims or Muslims. And fundamentally an Arab-Muslim is a Sunni not a Shi'ite, or a Shi'ite not a Sunni. Arab history is one of constant war.

H: You are highlighting what I picked up in my reading without daring to think it. The first Arab-Muslim society began to enrich itself through conquests, not from the time of the caliphate, but even earlier. The Prophet conducted wars and grew richer with each victory. The spoils were enormous. The earliest Muslim society enriched itself in this way. Later the first great *fitna* (war between Muslims) broke out because 'Uthmān plundered the public treasury to enrich his clan.

A: 'Uthmān, as all historians agree, spent enormous sums on enriching his family with no regard to the wider community. You're right to talk about enrichment through war and conquest, because Islam's fortune came from *ghanā'im* (spoils of war). From the start Islam adopted the violence of wars and conquests.

H: Apart from the *ghanā'im*, there was the tribute paid by non-Muslims or those who wanted to keep their own religions. Women were part of the spoils. They were kept or sold as captives of war.

A: Historically, Islam, as I said earlier, was founded on the tribal mentality, conquests and the power of money. Today, Daesh is enriching itself thanks to *ghanā'im* and control of oil and gas supplies, money from banks and the sale of women . . .

H: Daesh extracts a tribute from non-Muslims, loots and takes women as captives of war, which is why I think that it repeats the dark side, not the enlightened side of the Mu'tazilites, the philosophers or the mystics.

A: But the Mu'tazilites did not form part of the Muslim institutional 'body'. Nor did the mystics, the philosophers or the poets.

H: The Mu'tazilites formed the most important current of opinion in Baghdad.

A: They were principally connected to one or two of the caliphs. The culture of the Mu'tazilites really took off in the era of the caliph al-Mā'mūn. But they were subjected to persecution and massacres from the time of the reign of the caliph al-Mutawakkil.

H: You said that the Arab intellectual has never been adopted by the political institution or encouraged by the powers that be. Since writing *Ath-thābit wa'l mutaḥawwil*, you have fought for freedom of speech.

A: That book arose from a process of questioning. Why can we not find a single great poet that we can identify as a Muslim believer? I know of no great poet who is a believer, nor any philosophers who were fully dogmatic believers. Neither Averroes, Avicenna[10] nor Rawandī[11] were really Muslim. Only Ghazālī, who became a mystic. So why is this civilization, which embraced mystics, philosophers and poets, which had no link with *fiqh* (jurisprudence) or

religious orthodoxy, called an Islamic or Muslim civilization? Muslim in what sense? What do the mystic or the
philosopher have to do with *fiqh* and *Sharia* (Law)? As a stu-
dent of the texts I have realized that there was no great poet
who could be designated a poet and a Muslim in the way
that Claudel was a poet and a Catholic Christian. I found
no Muslim thinkers or philosophers who could match the
figure of Emmanuel Levinas, the philosopher and Jewish
believer. Reading the works of history, I constantly asked
myself this question: why wasn't the poetic tradition instituted by Islam founded on creativity and imagination rather
than on things that remained closely allied to religion and
power? And to conclude, why have Arab countries neglected
teaching about the great poets? The great poets have not
been correctly taught.

H: Even al-Mutanabbī?

A: He was badly taught. School pupils and students knew
only a few poems. On the other hand, the poetical world of
al-Mutanabbī, like that of the other great poets, remained
unknown because it was neglected or badly understood. So
I decided to undertake this work in order to rethink this tradition and write another history. I have done no more than
open a horizon for research.

H: But no one followed in your footsteps.

A: Unfortunately. But I think that currently a more
questioning mentality is beginning to emerge.

H: When I said that no one followed in your footsteps, I meant that there wasn't a generation coming after you who would pursue that questioning further. In the way that the generation of Moustapha Safouan came after that of Moustapha Ziwar[12] or Taha Hussein.

A: In literary circles people are beginning to be interested in this way of reading history. Younger writers are starting to apply themselves to the task. *Ath-thābit wa'l mutaḥawwil* has been through many editions. It has become a classic of literary history. It is currently in its fifteenth edition. In intellectual circles, there is an increasing clamour for a greater freedom of thought. However, we need to go further. This was just a beginning. We now have to interrogate the foundations of Islam and the underlying basis of this culture that we call Islamic culture. In any case, at present, we are pained to admit that the Islam advocated by fundamentalism is a religion without culture. Moreover, the Arabs are ignorant of their corpus and their sources.

H: The question then is: when you have read Hegel, Marx, Heidegger, Kant, Lacan, Foucault, the Greeks, etc. – as have certain great Arab intellectuals such as Moustapha Safouan – can you still be interested in Tabarī or Ibn Kathīr? Maybe this ignorance of our culture stems from this: the intellectual universe we are discovering is so vast that we can no longer immerse ourselves in this theological corpus of days gone by.

A: I totally agree. But I would add and emphasize again that there is no Arab culture today.

H: How do you mean?

A: In the sense that there is no creative Arab culture that participates in changing the world. While we can talk about a French or American culture because there are French or American problematics, we cannot argue that there is a vision of the world that is profoundly Arab. There is no Arab problematic because Islam has dominated the vision of the Arab world. Muslims see the world through the Islamic vision, which is ancient and closed. Islam has no need of the world, of the other, of culture, because it is the absolute Culture. It is unchanging and will remain so until the end of time. What innovation has it ever produced in relation to ancient civilizations?

H: Perhaps a way of building the Arab story and an Arab philosophy which attempted to reconcile religion with Greek culture and, in the end, mysticism.

A: But I am speaking of the present. And we mustn't forget that mysticism has always been marginalized in Muslim culture. Even the attempts to reconcile philosophy and religion came to a halt a long time ago.

H: Mysticism – like philosophy – was not well regarded by orthodox theologians and jurists. But it formed part of the intellectual fabric of Arab society, even if the mystics aren't read any more today, any more than the philosophers, for that matter.

A: That's why I said that the Arabs didn't know their own sources or their own corpus. And although their vision remains fundamentally a religious one, they don't even read their Book. They are to a distressing degree ignorant of the language of their foundational text.

H: How is it that the majority of intellectuals who are familiar with the Enlightenment and Western philosophy don't manage to think beyond the religious view of the world?

A: Fear, mainly. Then because thinking, in Arab society, is tantamount to declaring war on that society. I would add that thought becomes a sort of function. And any thinker who is a functionary lives in fear. We have to admit also that there are no great geniuses in our society. There isn't a single writer who has asked fundamental questions concerning religion, God, belief, existence, art, language . . . Writers don't ask any questions about our traditions, our culture. The only literature in existence is a literature of repetition.

H: Can genius exist in a society where we sup fear with our mother's milk and where thought is constantly condemned, where we run the risk of being banished, even persecuted, as soon as we start to interrogate our corpus or our heritage?

A: It's an extremely complex problem. There are all sorts of snares. One of them merits repeating: those who have read Western philosophers and have familiarized themselves with Western thought are no longer part of the Arab cultural body. They have fallen between European culture and their allegiance to a country in which they are neither known nor recognized.

H: The Arab intellectual suffers doubly. Exiled doubly. Banished doubly.

A: Our culture, even today, opposes and condemns anything that is different. The thinker who wants to repudiate the classical vision promulgated by religion is no longer allowed to be part of the community. He is accused of treason and apostasy. The individual thus lives in a society that reduces him to a mere appurtenance. It's an historical problem: what we call 'Islam' has not respected the diversity of Arab society itself. It attacked art and tried to destroy all the beauty that pre-existed it. But art cannot be reduced to merely a means of decorating a house or composing a song; art is a vision of the world and a relationship with the world.

H: When the Qur'an speaks of an earlier time, it calls it the *jāhilīya*, the time of ignorance. It displays a contempt for, and a denial of, civilizations that pre-dated it: the Persian, Pharaonic and Mesopotamian civilizations. Arguably, it marked a backward step, in social terms, compared with Roman society.

A: Muslim culture is one of decadence when you compare it to what went before. Islam grew up in the heart of a tribal culture based on commerce and power. We all know that the founding fathers were all merchants: Khadīja, Muhammad's first wife, was a merchant. Abū Bakr,[13] 'Umar[14] and 'Uthmān were also merchants. In fact, it wasn't a step back only in relation to the Romans, but relative to contemporary Arab society. In Arabia there was the figure of Sajār, who was the chief of his tribe. Before the advent of Islam, women were free and could fulfil important roles in their society. As for Mecca, it was the birthplace of the *Mu'allaqāt*,[15] which I personally regard as a truly universal poetry. The fact that the Revelation chose the language of the *Mu'allaqāt* shows the true grandeur of the latter. Arabs have a duty to rethink their history.

H: Taha Hussein did something extraordinary when he asked questions about pre-Islamic poetry. The judges who condemned him knew perfectly well that poetry was seen in a poor light by Islam. Logically, they should have applauded. But the state condemned him and refuted his theses. In fact, thought itself was the target. It wasn't so much a love of pre-Islamic poetry as a hatred of thought and innovation.

A: Exactly. I will take this opportunity to state that pre-Islamic poetry is a poetry of thought, love and subjectivity. The simple fact that the Revelation chose a language that pre-existed it proves that this language was endowed with a grandeur and infinite richness, as I have just said. But commerce triumphed, and an army proved victorious. In victory, it enriched itself; by enriching itself, it conquered the world. It should be added that Islam did not have to face any serious opposition at the beginning. For example, Syria did not wage war on Islam. Baghdad, Damascus and Egypt welcomed Muslims, because they had been bled dry by the Byzantine Empire.

H: I would like to add one thing about the customs of the times. Islam fought against the Christians as it did against all other religions. But the first Muslims who sought refuge in Abyssinia in order to escape the mistreatment of the Meccans found a protector in the person of King Najāshī, who was a Christian. He offered them asylum and the freedom to practise their religion.

A: And this exile in Abyssinia saved the first Muslims. Nevertheless, the Christians were later disavowed and opposed. I would add this: imprisoned in a very closed vision of religion, those who exercised power and led their countries never managed to constitute a society or a state based on citizenship and equality. From the very beginning to the present day.

H: Freud links the construction of Judaism with the construction of the figure of Moses. He was an Egyptian who sought to lead the Hebrews out of slavery. There are two observations here: firstly, the foundational figure is a foreigner; secondly, the people cling to a belief out of a love of freedom. We, on the other hand, from the beginning have only talked about the tribe and loyalty to the tribe or the family.

A: By touting Islam as the absolute solution, the Islamic vision has eradicated existential problems such as love, death and freedom. Thus death, love and freedom are considered or defined only within a strictly religious framework. Any other way of addressing them is seen as heretical or infidel.

H: Islam needs to be rethought. The difference with Judaism and Christianity is in the absence of the murder of the founder. And you say in *Al Kitāb*: Muʿāwīya, Abū Bakr, ʿUthmān, ʿAlī . . . are not dead. Yet death is the foundation of all discourse. We can't talk about a history liberated from death.

A: There is no thought of death or any other problematic. As for the language of the Qurʾan, it is beautiful, but it is rhetorical and impersonal. On the other hand, the language of the poets is intrinsically linked to human experience. It is more vivid, imaginative and personal. The Arab poets approached the language of the Qurʾan from an aesthetic point of view, as forming part of a linguistic world that existed even before the advent of Islam. The language of ʿImruʾu l-Qays remains beautiful and powerful, even in translation.

H: I now better understand Moustapha Safouan's thoughts on vernacular languages.[16] If you translate the Qurʾan into vernacular language, what is left?

A: That is why we are told to translate the meanings of the Qurʾan rather than its language. Some literary critics, when they speak about the inimitability of the Qurʾan, are talking about its meanings and not the language. From this point of view, you can find poetry or prose texts endowed with a beauty just as great as that of the text of the Qurʾan, especially the Suras of Medina. Nevertheless, no Arab poet or writer has tried to imitate the language of the Qurʾan.

31

Rethinking the Fundamentals

H: Mesopotamia was the cradle of two great civilizations: the Sumerian and the Babylonian. This land witnessed the birth of writing, of gods and of the stories that would be taken up later by the Old Testament and the Qur'an. How do we explain the triumph of monotheism?

A: I think monotheism is the result of two things. Firstly, the development of a sense of the economic sphere. Secondly, the development of a sense of power. These two elements revolutionized the ancient world, the place of great polytheistic civilizations, and killed the idea of plurality.

H: Let's begin with the idea of the gods.

A: A single power in heaven and a single representative on earth. This monotheist thesis bears witness to the triumph of the economic sphere and of power on earth. Islam is the final example of this.

H: If I understand correctly, religious power has transformed itself into a social and political exercise of authority. 'A single authority' in all areas of life.

A: In fact, power has transformed everything. Islam was born in a place of commerce, Mecca. This society of merchants needed a single leader so that the spirit of commerce could triumph. It was a society that wanted to unite the tribes under the standard of a single power.

H: At the same time, this indicates a great force. Mecca was effectively a commercial crossroads. But to feed itself it depended on other towns, in present-day Yemen, such as Al-Yamāma and Sanaa, which supplied it with grain and other produce.

A: Commerce was triumphant because the ancient world was by now old. The Byzantines left behind an empty world. Syria opened its doors to Muslims. Worn down by the Byzantines, the people of Damascus, the majority of whom were oppressed Nestorians, thought that the Muslims were their saviours. They welcomed them with open arms. The Muslims enriched themselves further with each victory. They became powerful thanks to their amassed wealth. You might even say that they were lucky, as they didn't have to face any real enemies or large armies. In the beginning the Arabs didn't wage real wars. In any case, there weren't any wars in the Greek or Roman sense.

H: It would be useful to reread these *Futūḥāt* (*The Conquests*). You invite us to analyse the socio-economic structure of the conquered countries.

A: *Futūḥ al-Buldān*[1] is a work of reference. In it we learn that war in the time of Muhammad was between tribes.

Once Arabia was unified, with a powerful army and rich leaders, whole countries, the real treasures of conquest, fell easily. Almost without resistance.

H: Marcus Aurelius had granted citizenship to so-called savage peoples. Islam came after other religions and other civilizations. But it didn't surpass them when it came to tolerance, respect for differences, the construction of a citizenship, the abolition of slavery . . .

A: On the contrary, Islam attacked the gains of preceding civilizations and of others that followed. But fundamentally it retained three things: the Bible, its Law and its Prophets. We might add to this magical thinking, which it transformed into a doctrine.

What does the foundational text say?

H: In *Les Tablettes babyloniennes*, Edward Chiéra writes: 'The thinking man is always interested in his past.'[2] Let us now reflect on the foundations of our religion, its principles and its vision of the world. It's more necessary today than ever.

A: Firstly, violence is a phenomenon common to all three monotheisms. Nevertheless, violence in the Bible is bound up with the history of a people which has known servitude and exile. In Christianity, violence goes hand in hand with the foundation of the Church. On the other hand, in Islam violence is specifically the violence of the conqueror.

H: When we read the works of history, such as the *Chronicles* of Tabarī, we realize that the Muslim religion was imposed by force and by violence.

A: The whole history shows this. Islam was imposed by force; it became a history of conquests. People had to convert or pay a tribute. So violence was part and parcel of the foundation of Islam.

H: In *Al-Kitāb* you talk about violence in the heart of the city after the death of Muhammad. But we are now going to broach a taboo subject: that of violence in the foundational text.

A: It is an extremely violent text. I have counted eighty verses on Gehenna. There are sixty verses evoking paradise and seventy-two that talk about paradise as a place of infinite pleasure. *Kufr* (unbelieving) and its consequences appear in 518 verses; torture and its consequences are the subject of more than 370 verses; 518 talk about punishment. Hell is mentioned eighty times. We can cite in particular: 'Whoever of you . . . dies while an unbeliever – these it is whose works shall go for nothing in this world and the hereafter, and they are the inmates of the fire; therein they shall abide.'[3] Yet there is not a single verse that urges reflection, nor any verse that discusses the benefits or advantages of reason or the spirit, in the sense of the creative spirit. When the Qur'an says *yatafakkarūn* (reflect, reason), it is in the sense of remembering the precepts indicated by the Qur'an and applying them.

H: Following this logic, anyone who has done good works and who dies an unbeliever will be a guest in Gehenna and will envy the fate of the believer who committed worse acts. To attenuate this nightmarish vision and to highlight the difference between the mystical text and the theological text, Ibn 'Arabī explains that *kufr* in Arab etymology means illusion or error of perception, not unbelieving.

A: Absolutely. But the theologian sees only unbelieving, and that merits punishment. In the case of 'unbelievers', the sentence is without appeal: 'Surely they who disbelieve in the communications of Allah they shall have a severe chastisement; and Allah is Mighty, the Lord of Retribution.'[4] The following verse is also worth citing: '(As for) those who disbelieve in Our communications, We shall make them enter fire; so oft as their skins are thoroughly burned, We will change them for other skins, that they may taste the chastisement.'[5]

H: I draw your attention to the fact that this verse on the removal of the skin and the attack on the 'self-skin' as a form of eternal torture appears in a Sura that has been named 'The Women'. From Tabarī to Fakhr al-Dīn al-Rāzī,[6] the commentators strove to make clear that the skin would be changed only in the case of eternal torture. Some said that it would be changed 70,000 times, others spoke of a torture without end.

A: Any individual Muslim who lives in a culture that vaunts torture is condemned to submit to the precepts of religion. Any deviation from the path defined by Islam is condemned. And Islam is the only acceptable religion. The following verse is instructive here: 'And whoever desires a religion other than Islam, it shall not be accepted from him.'[7] And again: 'This day have I perfected for you your religion and completed My favour on you and chosen for you Islam as a religion.'[8] There is a theoretical violence and a practical violence in the Text. The former has engendered the latter. On the practical level, for example, an individual is not allowed to replace the faith of his family or community with another one.

H: Many verses condemn apostasy, which is in fact the choice of an individual and his freedom to take a different path from that of his family or his community. Religion refuses that choice. Here on earth, that individual runs the risk of being beheaded, while in the hereafter God reserves for him an exemplary punishment.

A: This brings to mind the following verse, which relates directly to this question: 'My Lord! leave not upon the land any dweller from among the unbelievers.'[9] The Muslim who reads this verse is invited to wage jihad to fulfil this wish and to combat 'unbelieving' with all the means at his disposal. It's a form of violence that is not seen as such because it is considered as a triumph of Islam and the divine will. Already we can say that violence is intrinsic to Islam. We can also quote: 'Therefore We inflicted retribution on them and drowned them in the sea';[10] 'On the day when We will seize (them) with the most violent seizing; surely We will inflict retribution';[11] 'We will gather them together on the day of resurrection on their faces, blind and dumb and deaf; their abode is hell; whenever it becomes allayed We will add to their burning.'[12]

H: In this same Sura we read: 'See how We have made some of them to excel others.'[13] It's the law of the arbitrary. Whether you choose the right way or go astray depends on the Lord, and thus on His arbitrary choice.

A: And those who do not enjoy the favour of the Lord find themselves described as follows: 'On the day when their faces shall be turned back into the fire',[14] or else: 'for them are cut out garments of fire, boiling water shall be poured over their heads. / With it shall be melted what is in their bellies and (their) skins as well. / And for them are whips of iron. / Whenever they will desire to go forth from it, from grief, they shall be turned back into it, and taste the chastisement of burning.'[15] Abū Hurayra quotes a *hadīth*[16] which explains this verse: 'Fire is poured into the skull. It crosses it and reaches the throat. It empties the throat and goes down as far as the feet. Then, he becomes as before.'[17] We might also cite the verse: 'Their shirts made of pitch and the fire covering their faces'.[18] Tabarī makes clear that the skin will burn 70,000 times each day.[19]

H: It's a terrifying image. The skin burns, falls off, is picked up, placed back on the body, is roasted, falls off again, is roasted again, and so on. This verse is terrifying because it cultivates masochism or a tyrannical superego, not to mention the terror that grips the individual, because touch is a very primitive sense. The skin is the first point of contact between a baby and its mother. And the mother's caresses on the skin of the baby introduce it to the world of autoeroticism which is so necessary for its psyche and its body. It is this primary skin that is attacked here.

A: Those who disobey, 'When the fetters and the chains shall be on their necks; they shall be dragged / Into boiling water, then in the fire shall they be burned.'[20]

H: The skin, the eyes and other orifices like the mouth or the nose are consumed by the fire. As well as what we have described already, the threat weighs on the sense of identity, as it is directed at the face. It is not just an organic suffering, but an attack on the very basis of human identity. This explains the terror involved in any questioning of the precepts or even the smallest movement of thought. If I think, I am literally risking my skin.

A: 'Lay hold on him, then put a chain on him, / Then cast him into the burning fire, / Then thrust him into a chain the length of which is seventy cubits.'[21] Some commentators describe the cord entering through the mouth of the tortured individual and exiting through the anus.[22]

H: And all this in such musical language, like a song or hymn to life. Those who don't read Arabic don't notice this discrepancy between the beauty of the language and the atrocious imagery of torture. This makes me think about *ānā ibn Jalā'*.[23] The Muslim who recites these verses is like someone who recites the lines of al-Ḥajjāj. The beautiful language expresses something nightmarish, and the musicality of the poetry is stained with blood. You recite terrible verses as if reading a love poem.

A: Everything is expressed with rhyme, in fact. We find ourselves facing the predominance of a sacred discourse: that of God, the One, backed up by the *faqīh*. Thought is invited to stand down, because the truth of the discourse does not reside in its inherent truth, but is based on the authority of the person who pronounces it. In anything to do with the divine, you simply have to believe.

H: Belief is intimately connected to terror. These tortures attack all the zones of the body: the skin, the stomach, the mouth, the erogenous zones, where self-preservation is connected to the libidinal. We know how fundamental the contact between mouth and breast is on the level of self-preservation and on the libidinal level.

A: Here, food and drink are diverted from their primary function to become instruments of torture. We can quote here: 'Surely with Us are heavy fetters and a flaming fire, / And food that chokes and a painful punishment.'[24]

H: Denise Masson attenuates the image when she translates *ghassa* as 'food that sticks in the throat'.

A: Ibn 'Abbās describes this torture by saying it is like a thorn in the throat that you can neither swallow nor spit out.[25]

H: Tabarī and Rāzī also pursue this line: that which serves as food threatening death.

A: Even the tree of nourishment becomes threatening. It is said: 'Surely the tree of the Zaqqum, / Is the food of the sinful / Like dregs of oil; it shall boil in (their) bellies, / Like the boiling of hot water.'[26]

H: Straight after this verse, God promises the best treatment to those who fear the Lord: 'Surely those who guard (against evil) are in a secure place, / In gardens and springs; / They shall wear of fine and thick silk.'[27]

A: The Qur'an talks about this tree in another Sura: 'Surely it is a tree that grows in the bottom of the hell; / Its produce is as it were the heads of the serpents'[28] and 'those who abide in the fire and who are made to drink boiling water so it rends their bowels asunder'.[29]

H: It follows the same logic. Just before this, it is written: 'A parable of the garden which those guarding (against evil) are promised: Therein are rivers of water that does not alter, and rivers of milk the taste whereof does not change, and rivers of drink delicious to those who drink, and rivers of honey clarified and for them therein are all fruits and protection from their Lord.'[30] So, reward or punishment.

A: The punishment is always cruel: 'This (shall be so); so let them taste it, boiling and intensely cold (drink).'[31]

H: 'Boiling drink' here translates *al-ghussāq*.

A: According to some commentators, it is molten iron that is poured on their skin. But according to 'Abdallah ibn 'Amrū, it is thick pus. If a single drop fell on the West, it would even pulverize the people of the East, he says, and if a drop fell on the East, it would completely obliterate the people of the West.[32] Ka'b adds: 'It's the very source of Gehenna. Every venomous animal, like the snake and the scorpion, comes to bathe in it. The individual is brought and thrown into the source. His skin and his flesh are loosened from his bones and fall off.'

H: I just want to draw attention to the fact that the term used in Ka'b's interpretation is *rajul*, man in the sense of a human individual. The commentator doesn't say: 'The miscreant is brought . . .'. The image does not relate solely to the non-believer, but to every human being. The threat becomes more effective; it packs a bigger punch.

A: These examples of torture are found throughout the Qur'an. Violence remains intrinsically connected with vengeance. It is the laws of the tribe transposed into the hereafter. The tortured person does not get to know death. 'It shall not be finished with them entirely so that they should die, nor shall the chastisement thereof be lightened to them: even thus do We inflict retribution on every ungrateful one.'[33] 'Surely (as for) those who disbelieve and act unjustly Allah will not forgive them nor guide them to a path / Except the path of hell, to abide in it for ever, and this is easy to Allah.'[34]

H: '*Khālidīna fīhā ābadān*, they will stay there for ever more'. This phrase appears in the Sura *An-nisā'* (The Women), where Gabriel threatens Hafsa and 'Ā'isha, the two wives of the Prophet, for having disobeyed their husband. And because they are wives of the Prophet, the punishment will be more terrible. In fact, all acts of disobedience incur a punishment down here and torture in the hereafter. The Qur'an portrays a Gehenna with an open maw.

A: God appears in the Qur'an as the 'Torturer' or the 'God of tortures' or the 'avenging God'. The places of torture are listed: *jahannam*, *saqar*, *lazā*, *hāwīya* (Gehenna, infernal fire, hell, the abyss). *An-nār* (the fire) is the means of extreme torture. The Qur'an attributes an identity and a voice to fire. The fire speaks of its insatiable appetite: 'On the day that We will say to hell: Are you filled up? And it will say: Are there any more?'[35]

H: There is a recourse to anthropomorphism and magical thinking, a childish form of thinking that doesn't yet distinguish between the animate and the inanimate. To give fire a voice and a mouth that devours reactivates infantile anxieties. The verse summons up those precocious stages of the psychic life which linger as traces. The verse is terrifying because it summons up that part of the repressed – but a living repressed. Both adult and child tremble in the face of the terrorizing imago.

A: All the more so as the Qur'an depicts the divinity with the attributes *Jabbār* (the Almighty) and *batsh* (oppression, tyranny).

H: It places the accent on the death-dealing and destructive aspect of the persecuting imago. Disobedience entails not simply a withdrawal of love but the chastisement of a vengeful god. Indeed, anyone who reads these verses and the commentaries that have been devoted to them experiences that feeling depicted by Dostoyevsky when he discussed Holbein's painting *The Body of the Dead Christ in the Tomb*: 'It could make a believer lose his faith.'

A: We have here a whole set of images of extreme cruelty. To this Qur'anic cruelty can be added that of the Muslims of the first century Hijri Era, in the year 622 AD. The first battle, at Badr, provided a very eloquent example. We might recall the statement of Ibn Mas'ūd, a companion of Muhammad, quoted by Ibn Hishām: 'O Messenger of God, it is the head of the enemy of God Abū Jahl.'[36]

H: In a number of works, including the *Tafsīr* (*Commentary*) of Tabarī and *As-sīra an-nabawīya* of Ibn Hishām, the angels join in battles and exterminate 'unbelievers'.

A: Tabarī recounts how God granted Muslims 3,000 angels[37] who decapitated the enemies of Muhammad at the battle of Badr. Abū Borda ibn Niyār, one of the combatants, made this remark: 'On the day of the battle of Badr I brought three heads and placed them before the prophet of God and said: "O Messenger of God! I chopped off the heads of the first two. However, the third was chopped off by a very tall white man, an angel who passed before an unbeliever. His head rolled. I picked it up."'[38] Al-Wāqidī also recounts that a lover, before being executed, asked to see the woman he loved. The woman was summoned and she arrived after the man had been beheaded. She showered him with kisses. Then she too was struck by death and died on the already cold body of her lover.[39]

H: Apart from the verses, the battles of Badr and Khaybar, there were other wars: *ḥurūb ar-rida*, known as the Wars of Apostasy, were quite merciless.

A: This was in the time of the first caliph, Abū Bakr. It wouldn't be inaccurate to call it a war of extermination. It was led by Khālid ibn al Walīd, who killed the poet Mālik ibn Nuwīra and took his wife in the year 12 Hijra (634 AD). It was said that the poet's head was used as a brazier. When 'Umar became caliph he condemned the act and punished Khālid ibn al Walīd. As for the War of the Camel, the battle of Siffin and the War of Nahrawān, these were conflicts of indescribable cruelty. They lasted five years and involved thousands of men, including companions of the Prophet, who were assured of paradise.

H: 'Umar, the second caliph and the father-in-law of the Prophet, is often presented as a major companion of Muhammad. But his violence is never discussed. Yet the story of him and Fāṭima, the daughter of the Prophet, is well known.

A: Some Muslims refused to pledge allegiance to Abū Bakr after the death of Muhammad. They gathered at the house of Fāṭima, the daughter of the Prophet. 'Umar called for their extermination. Then he went to Fāṭima's house with the intention of burning it down. She said: 'Have you come to burn down our house?' He said: 'Yes, unless you say the same thing as the rest of the community.'

H: He struck Fāṭima, who was pregnant. She had a miscarriage which cost her her life.

A: Arab history is very complex and extremely violent. But from 41 Hijra, that is the reign of Mu'āwīya in Damascus, violence became a religious, cultural, political and social structure. This has been the hegemonic structure – up to the present day.

H: The violence is expressed in the verses, in the poems or in the speeches of monarchs. By being wedded to language it has become sacred.

A: Violence needs a sacred character because it defends the sacred. Mu'āwīya, the first Umayyad caliph, used to say: 'Earth belongs to God, and I am His caliph. That which I take from men belongs to me. What I leave behind is out of generosity.' Or else: 'I don't interfere with people's language as long as they don't interfere with our reign.' 'Abd al-Malik ibn Marwān, another Umayyad caliph, said after his coronation: 'I swear that I will behead anyone who asks me to be pious.' He also said: 'My only remedy for the ills of this community is my sword.' He told his son: 'Summon the people after my death so that they might swear allegiance to you. Cut off the heads of any who refuse.'

H: Al-Ḥajjāj ibn Yūsuf al-Thaqāfī was renowned for his great cruelty. He threatened the Iraqis with beheading in verses that have become very famous. We recite his verses and praise his language without paying attention to the threat of decapitation. Later, the Abbassids would rival the Umayyads when it came to violence.

A: How can we forget the words of Abū Ja'far al-Manṣūr, the founder of the Abbassid dynasty? He said: 'The blood of anyone who refutes our allegiance is licit.' And he addressed this message to his son al-Mahdī: 'There are three categories of men: the poor man who hopes for your help, the man who fears you and seeks your protection and the prisoner who awaits your clemency.' All these quotes point to a violence intrinsic in the exercise of power, whether this power is legitimate or usurped. The monarch had legislative, executive and judicial power.

H: All those who exercised power, whether the first caliphs, the Umayyads or the Abbassids, did so in the name of religion.

A: Religion was no more than a means of exercising power. And money has always served the interests of the governors. True, over the course of history, there have been examples that run counter to this despotism, just as there are certain verses that call for mercy. But Muslims have opted for the general rule. They have preferred to respond to the instinct of domination and cruelty at the expense of justice, equality and the sense of sharing. I'd like to add that torture took different forms. The Iraqi historian 'Abbūd al-Shaljī, in his work *Mawsū'at al-'adhāb* (*The Encyclopaedia of Tortures*), recorded 200. Among them were: death by spearing with a lance, suffocation, burial alive, burning alive, being thrown into a vat of boiling water, being scorched alive, the body being dragged . . .

H: In *Al-Kitāb* I was fascinated by those tortures that destroyed the being. While translating it, I had great difficulty finding words to express crucifixion, dismemberment . . . and I discovered by reading you that women were tortured too.

A: Torture was physical and/or psychological. Mu'āwīya imprisoned 'Amrū ibn al-Haqq al-Khuzā'ī (a partisan of 'Alī) as well as his wife. They beheaded the man and ordered that he be placed on his wife's knees. Hishām ibn 'Abd al-Mālik ordered the beheading of Zayd ibn 'Alī. They placed his head on the knees of his mother. Marwān, nicknamed 'al-Himār' (the ass), the last of the Umayyads, was beheaded and his head placed on the knees of his daughter. Ziyad ibn Abīh was in the habit of dismembering women before he killed them. It amused him to crucify the woman completely naked. The Abbassid caliph ordered that a woman should be thrown to the big cats. She was devoured. This is what Suyūtī tells us in *Nuzhat al-majālis*.[40]

H: Suyūtī is the one who talks about a rod in the hereafter that never bends. The title you mentioned displays a pleasure in sadism: *Nuzhat* here means 'rejoicing'. There is a contradiction between the content (torture) and the title (rejoicing). There is a double violence here: the violence that is practised and another which it calls other than by its name. And *majālis*, which evokes 'banquet', 'boudoir', 'gathering', can't fail but evoke the structure of sadism.

A: That was the case for the woman tortured by 'Ubaydallāh. He cut off her foot and said to her: 'What do you think of that?' She said: 'I am busy with something else.' He broke her other foot. She placed her hand on her sex. He said: 'Are you protecting it?' She replied: 'Your mother didn't protect it.' We can also cite the example of the Turkish governor in 1098 who habitually bound women he didn't like in a bundle of clothes or locked them in a chest and threw them in the River Al-'Āṣṣī. Sometimes the torture bordered on madness: al-Qāhir tortured his mother-in-law and hung her by her breasts. Sometimes torture followed accusations of illicit love, as in the case of an Egyptian woman suspected of being involved in a love affair with a Christian. She was stripped naked and tied to the tail of an ass, which dragged her to her death. This story appears in *Badī' az-zuhūr*.

H: 'Marvel of flowers'. I don't think these tortures that crop up throughout the history of the Arabs have been studied in the light of psychoanalysis. The Sadean hero says: 'I know only my own pleasure and to achieve it I torture and I kill.' The one who commits the torture experiences pleasure. These stories have been passed down but never analysed. We have a legacy stained with blood and horror with no way of thinking about it.

A: We do indeed lack a psychoanalytical study. We need to analyse this vision of man and the world which is imprinted with violence and cruelty. And we should recall that there is both a practical violence, the one we have just described, and another, which is subjacent to it. History attests to one fact: it is the Muslim vision that possesses man, not vice versa. Once history is sacralized, we have no means of studying the personality of Muhammad as we do for other prophets of monotheism. Anyone who tries to do so or expresses a desire to do so exposes himself to the accusation of apostasy.

H: In *Moses and Monotheism*, Freud developed a veritable dismantling of the founding father, revealing to what extent the murder of the father is necessary. Muhammad remains idealized and sacralized. And all his actions and gestures are regarded as rules to be followed. Unchangeable rules. Moreover, many of the legends to do with him are considered as incontrovertible truth.

A: The texts are in agreement that the Prophet Muhammad was perfect as a Prophet and not as a man. In spite of that he continues to be sacralized, and history has greatly contributed to this sacralization. The Sudanese writer Mohamed Mahmoud relates a certain number of stories that appear in the works of hagiography. For example, Muhammad was said to have had an 'excrescence' between his shoulders 'like an apple or an egg'. So this problem had to be dealt with. In other words, the ultimate prophet couldn't be allowed to have a deformity. So the conclusion was that it was a tangible proof of ultimate prophetic status.

H: In the light of this story we can reflect on form, image and model, as did Louis Marin in his discussion of Jesus as Image.

We might also recall Moses, who was not eloquent. Should we take this phrase literally or figuratively? In fact, these are questions that can be tackled from a theological, philosophical or anthropological point of view. But we can't do it.

A: This violence does not annul simply the spirit, but also the human range of the Muslim. A Muslim is obliged to believe without asking any question of the Prophet, whether on a religious, intellectual or social level. In this respect, violence becomes sacred. History is also created by God and the Prophet. It is not written by the Muslims. Consequently, it too becomes divine. And within this history, the good is that which is admitted by Islam, and the bad is that which is refused, without any respect for what is permitted or forbidden by other peoples. What this boils down to is a violence in relation to others.

H: Which perhaps explains the absence of 'the other as structure', in the expression of Gilles Deleuze, in the vision of the monarch which derives its authority from the religious vision.

A: The other has to be annulled as other. This is where the violence of the jihad springs from. The murder of the other is a jihad. In this respect, it becomes sacred. It leads the assassin to paradise, the place of quietude and pleasure. Eros and Thanatos are united in the jihad.

H: Unless we say: Thanatos, or the death drive, allies itself with Eros only in order to tear it from the libidinal. Pleasure is a figure of the death-bringer.

A: Jihad liberates the instincts. This violence compromises the humanity of man. If war, according to Heraclitus, 'is the father and king of all', the fact remains that, in our history, it has been present from the start. Could death in jihad be a reprise of these legends of the beginning?

H: A beginning conveniently unstudied and unanalysed. However, there is more and more written these days about a spiritual or moderate form of Islam. Some authors propound an Islam that has nothing to do with violence. It's to do with a difficulty in facing up to the underlying drives in the foundation of Islam. Most Muslims have not read their history correctly.

A: If you really want to understand Islam properly, read *The Book of Conquests* by al-Wāqidī. I also recommend the book by Mohamed Mahmoud entitled *The Prophecy of Muhammad: The Story of Its Conception*. It's one of the most important works in contemporary Arab culture. I've learned so much from it. I recommend anyone working on Islam to read it. It is a violence that terrorizes the human. Islam judges and condemns the human being, who must not know anything, experiment with anything, except what the divine precepts say. Consequently, man is not only a follower (*tābi'*), but also a slave.

H: Following this logic, instead of liberating man, religion reinforces the feeling of servitude. Religion thus turns out to be even more disastrous than 'the opiate of the people' defined by Marx.

A: Religion is synonymous with enclosure and imprisonment. When the Text speaks of tolerance, when it evokes *rah
ma* (mercy), it adds another condition: absolute submission
to Islam and its precepts. That's the price of mercy.

H: It's not the Christian *agape*.

A: Not at all. Man must show he is a vassal. It is this vassal-
age that will save him on the Day of Judgement. His salvation
rests on this absolute submission. It should be added that we
do not find any questioning of what it is to be human, of
existential anguish, of what is repressed in this culture, of
what the future of this culture might be. Everything is con-
centrated on a wretched discourse which reduces politics to
the fall of a regime, whatever the price that must be paid.

H: D. H. Lawrence, in his reading of the Apocalypse of
Saint John,[41] points out that there is a private domain of religion (which is Christ, the man of goodness and love), and a
wild and popular domain, the Apocalypse, which he defines
as the 'book of Zombies'.[42] When you evoked that time or
space between life and death I thought about those zombies.
The problem is that it is not the private book that triumphed
in the eyes of Muslims but the second one. Why is it that
Muslim intellectuals are unable to do this type of reading?

A: Traditional Islamic thought has always displayed hostility and hatred towards philosophy. We are returning to
the notion of violence as history, as thought, as practice
and as a vision of the world. Philosophical reflection has no
place here because Revelation, as I have said many times,

stipulates that the Prophet of the Muslims is the ultimate prophet, that he speaks definitive truths, and that humans have nothing more to say or to add. And if we pursue this line of reasoning, we can say that God has nothing more to say or to add to what He has already formulated because He has said His last Word to His last Prophet. From the point of view of culture: 1) There is only one God: the God of Islam. 2) It is He who makes and gives form. Thus He is the sole Creator. 3) There is only one book: the Qur'an. 4) There is only one universe: that of the Muslims. No place for other faiths or other believers within Muslim society. 5) The world must be Islamicized, because only one religion exists, and that is Islam. Further, when you say 'There is only one god', it's not just a question of any old god. It is the god of the Muslims. There is a single god as he exists in a single cultural universe. Individuals who live in it must be Muslims or they are condemned as renegades. Yet the rejection of the other, the non-believer, means that there is no equality. So we have to preach equality not tolerance. Plurality is precious. In the beginning was plurality, not the One. The One springs from ideology.

H: When the Qur'an accuses other monotheist religions of having falsified the Text, without specifying what it is that they have falsified, it attacks the so-called religions of the Book. This constitutes a violence in respect of other monotheist religions.

A: There are many studies of the Bible and of Christianity. But not of Islam.

H: We can also identify this violence in relation to earlier civilizations. Islam doesn't recognize them. The religious institution refused constructive comparisons, or what we would now call the science of civilization, in other words a comparative approach which uncovers the richness of cultural experiences and the diversity of each civilization.

A: Just as it doesn't recognize the notion of the subject or free individual.

H: You wrote an article on this question which was published in the Acts of the conference on 'The Psyche and the Arabs' in 2004.[43] And you took up the question again at the CIRET[44] congress, organized by Basarab Nicolescu in 2015 at the Collège des Bernadins.

A: I was exploring problems of subjectivity within the Salafi Islamic culture. I was arguing that the self of the individual was not determined by his interior world, but by the Text and the consensus of the community. The self is therefore not a true space for self-movement and creativity. The self is dissolved into the community. The latter becomes a sort of machine that crushes the freedom of the individual. Man is born within Islamic culture like a full stop or a fixed word in a book that is the Ummah (community). The consciousness of the individual is asked to play just a single role: to follow the divine text. The individual becomes the prisoner of the Text. Heraclitus said: 'A man's character is his demon', that is, his internal, free potential. And the first message of religion consists in killing this internal demon.

H: But the demon may be the free and creative part of the individual.

A: The truth of the world does not lie in the world but in the so-called universal Text. And the individual must obey the Text and the community, which accepts no divergence from the Text. I also say that the Arab lives in 'two prisons', following the expression of Abū l-'Alā'al-Ma'arrī: that of the Salafi interpretation of the religious text and that of the dissolution of his self in the Ummah, the community.

H: Freedom seems a long way off. How do we reach it? I feel that we are faced with Kafka's *The Castle*.

A: From a historic, scientific and human point of view, truth cannot be singular. It is plural and complex. And even if we agree that God is One in a singular heaven, believers are multiple and different in the exercise of their beliefs. Everyone has their own truth. It is in the plurality of religions, cultures and ideas that the meaning of the human and of the universe resides. To enclose cultures and religions in a sole religion and a sole culture on the pretext of bringing them to fulfilment is an act of aggression against both humanity and truth.

H: Punishment is meted out to anyone who calls for freedom from the totalitarian side of religion. In the name of the Qur'an, dialogue with a different other is not accepted.

A: What is overlooked is that God Himself dialogued with Satan. But these days, all dialogue is refused. This refusal to discuss is a form of enclosure, an enclosure that constitutes a genuine violence. The individual must remain inside the circle drawn by the precepts. Anyone with different beliefs is threatened here on earth and in the hereafter. Today, those who use violence and take up arms on the pretext of defending their truth or imposing it by use of force on others in fact end up doing nothing more than destroying everything by destroying freedom. Also, the first step would be to liberate research from all shackles and from the violence that weighs down on it in the Arab world, directly or indirectly. Because a society where truths cannot freely be stated is a society of servitude.

H: Hannah Arendt wrote: 'No thought without freedom'.

A: There is no existence without freedom. To deprive man of his freedom is to deprive him of his language. And if we say that language is a means of expression, how might the Arab express his freedom when he is deprived of his personal language? How can impersonal, non-individual language reflect the consciousness of a person?

H: The Book of Revelation is a text with many levels. There is John writing about Jesus as noble, cultivated, individual and kind. Then there is the book full of hatred. D. H. Lawrence, in his short book *Apocalypse*, pays homage not to Jesus but to Judas, saying that, without the tragedy of Judas, Jesus would not have been Jesus. So there is this subtle point that leads Lawrence to say that people who pray to Jesus are in fact paying homage to Judas. In Islam we lack this sort of reading.

A: Because of the interdiction weighing down on thought. You aren't allowed to think, to question. The Text can never be subjected to criticism or controversy. Moreover, the Text is repeated on a daily basis as a history that Muslims tell themselves, all the while living outside of themselves. They become 'followers' in order to live according to the sacred code, which is a prohibitive code.

H: The Qur'an, which came after Christianity, did not take from Christianity the goodness of Jesus but rather the hatred of the Book of Revelation. Revelation is the book or ultimate power, according to Gilles Deleuze, which doesn't embrace plurality because it is the power without appeal of a god who judges all the other powers.

A: I totally agree with Gilles Deleuze. He is absolutely right. If we look at the historical experience, we can say, on a practical level, Islam was more an exercise of power than a design for a new humanity. It is not a religion of knowledge, of research, of questioning, of individual flourishing. It is a religion of power. Modern-day Islam is a prime example of this.

H: Today, Daesh, in order to extend its power, seizes control of gas and oil fields and also grows rich on the sale of pills for jihadists. Once again: money and sexuality.

A: It is an incarnation of the violence of the past. No progress, because progress has already happened. It has taken place once and for all. That was at the moment of Revelation. It is written in the Qur'an: 'Islam is the sole religion', according to the dominant reading of the Qur'anic text. We thus have to live this Revelation, which incarnates the ultimate progress in the history of humanity. To say that it is the incarnation of the past with its catalogue of violence is the same as saying that Islam is not a message of liberation but an appeal to servitude, to perpetual war in order to Islamicize humanity.

H: I think it is not about a return of the repressed but a return of the split, in other words, of that violence since the beginning of the foundation which has not been thought and which remains encysted by the sacralization of everything connected to the Muslim religion and its foundation. That part that has been encysted returns in this form (violence) in order to question that which has not benefited from a genuine process of thought.

A: You have expressed that well. Those who have tried to think or introduce a thought have been ostracized or attacked, like the mystics, philosophers and poets. They thought, interpreted, employed the power of reasoning and creativity, but they were banished or assassinated.

H: I come back to Gilles Deleuze. He speaks of a monstrous time when he evokes the Book of Revelation. For Christ's message decided in favour of a presence and an eternity in life. You have often spoken about a 'more than life', an eternity that is simply the eternity of life.

A: Absolutely. Everything was thrown out of kilter by the birth of the institution of the Church. But in Islam there is a total absence of the human as human and an annulment of the self. The revolutions of today preach an ascension to heaven or a fall into Gehenna.

H: In *Beginnings of the Body, Ends of the Sea*, you evoke *janna* (paradise) in a very subtle fashion. When I think of *janna* and its attendant rivers of honey, its *houris*, its cup-bearers, as described in the texts of the hagiographers, I find these images impoverished, mean even. A man reading these texts rejoices because he is condemned to spend eternity drinking, eating and copulating. Where is the spirituality in this?

A: If God condemns humans to drinking, eating and copulating, He must really detest the human.

H: As if man were not a creature of culture. In fact, it's the notion of sublimation that needs to be raised.

A: The notion of culture is missing, as indeed is the very notion of nature. Nature is absent from the Islamic vision. I wonder if that is the reason we note the lack at the heart of Muslim monotheism of two dimensions (*bu'd*): the aesthetic and the scientific.

H: And that is . . .?

A: Nature is by definition the location of plurality. But this nature is absent from the Islamic vision, which is focused exclusively on the idea of absolute unity. Since beauty resides in the One and His word, knowledge does not come from nature but from the One who knows everything and is the source of all knowledge. Knowledge and learning are contained in the Revelation. I would even add that the ban on representation comes from the absence of a plural nature. And the degradation of women derives from this absence of nature. But woman is the noblest image of nature.

H: You are inviting us to reconsider the ban on representation preached by the Old Testament and repeated by the Qur'an.

A: We note this absence in the language itself; that is, the word becomes the unique property of God or the Revelation. Hence the importance of *fiqh* (jurisprudence), which has transformed the world into words, thus projecting the man of the world and of nature towards the world of language. *Fiqh* has annihilated the rights of the individual through recourse to the idea of the licit and the illicit, setting limits to the very idea of freedom and tracing the conditions for knowledge. Thus culture becomes a simple 'instruction' beneath the banner of the law. Life itself ends up reduced to a world of prohibitions and interdicts. So we can't liberate ourselves in the Arab world unless we break with *fiqh*. It has created in the heart of Islam an extremely narrow and impoverished vision, historically linked to the exercise of power. *Fiqh* was neither a liberation nor an exploration of philosophical or scientific horizons, but rather a judicial school that followed and justified the political power of the caliphate.

H: A text by André Malraux, dated 3 June 1956, says the following: 'The violence of the Islamic upsurge is a major phenomenon of our times. Underestimated by the majority of our contemporaries [. . .] today the Western world seems ill prepared to face the problem of Islam.'

A: However, we should make clear that he was talking about Arab Islam. I have just come back from Kerala in India. I was very conscious of the religious pluralism there. Their society is made up of Hindus, who constitute about 60 per cent of the inhabitants, Muslims and Christians. People are aware of this pluralism and defend it. Talking with Hindus, Christians and Muslims, I sensed and noted that the Muslims were part of the social fabric. Having said that, the mentality of Arab Islam is starting to infiltrate and spread. In this part of the world, women never used to be veiled. Now you see more and more girls and women wearing the veil. This speaks volumes about the Saudi influence which is starting to invade the public space.

Women and the twists and turns of the Text

H: 'Now I would like to recount that dream in verse, the better to delight your hearts, for Love begs and commands me to do so. And if any man or woman should ask me what I wish this romance, which I now begin, to be called, it is the *Romance of the Rose*, in which the whole art of Love is contained. The matter is fair and new; God grant that she for whom I have undertaken it may receive it with pleasure, She it is who is so precious and so worthy of being loved that she ought to be called Rose.'[45]

In *Beginnings of the Body, Ends of the Sea*, the woman makes a majestic entrance. Poetry remains the ally of the feminine and of women.

A: Poetically speaking, the universe is feminine.

H: The Arab corpus preciously retains the names of rebel or pioneer women. It is Rābi'a[46] who provided beacons for the path of Muslim mysticism. Fāṭima reminded us that the Prophet was a mortal among mortals. 'Ā'isha[47] not only transgressed the verse which asked the wives of the Prophet to stay at home,[48] but she also led a war.

A: Because women have always been discredited or banished, when not literally crushed. They are never among the leaders. They are always in the second tier. They formed no part of what fundamentally constituted a society. They were regarded as merely decorative. This has created in them a consciousness of injustice and a feeling of revolt. However, deprived of work and autonomy, they have not often had the chance to express their opposition to a system that degrades them. Nevertheless, there are revolutionary figures such as the women you mentioned: 'Ā'isha, Fāṭima, Rābi'a and especially Sajāḥ. Sajāḥ was the strongest, because she was the chief of a tribe. She exercised power.

H: I didn't know about her until I read *Al-Kitāb*, and not many texts afford her her proper place. She is bound up with other women chiefs such as Bilqīs, the queen of Saba'. In defiance of Mecca and Medina, she made a marriage of pure love and pure desire. She fascinates you. You devoted a magnificent poem to her in the first volume of *Al-Kitāb*.[49]

A: She demanded an extraordinary dowry: that the marriage should free her from religion and the weight of tradition. It is as if she was saying to Musaylima, her future husband: 'I will agree to marry you on the condition that you free me from the chains of religion. Our marriage has nothing to do with religion.' That is superb!

H: In effect, she broke with tradition. By refusing a dowry, she expressed her desire not to be bought. As a wise chief, she negotiated on behalf of her people the quantities of grain that Al-Yamāma, Musaylima's town, should give to its people. We should add that she reigned over four tribes. Among the men under her command were her uncles. The men in her tribe were in no way humiliated by having a woman ruler.

A: One of the essential conditions for a revolution is that it should keep as far as possible away from everything religious. The encounter of Sajāḥ and Musaylima was an encounter of a man and a woman. It was a form of secularity beyond religion and its precepts and conditions.

H: Are you saying that the sexual coupling is in itself secular?

A: She could see beyond religion. Sajāḥ's experience occurred at the point when Islam was starting to predominate. She disavowed the rules of Islam.

H: Or a mode of being. ʿĀʾisha also transgressed the rules established by her husband, the Prophet. Rābiʿa was the first, before al-Ḥallāj,[50] to ask for the destruction of the Kaʿba in favour of a spirituality liberated from all dogma.

A: In fact, all these women stood up against the precepts of Islam, as demonstrated by their works. Nevertheless, we shouldn't minimize the support of their partners. ʿĀʾisha and Sajāḥ were aided by men. They joined this revolution, which was founded on the intimate and free relationship between women and men. The men who agreed to join the revolt of these women and helped sustain revolutionary femininity were part of this femininity. Femininity is something that goes beyond women. It is a sort of intimate encounter between two human beings, irrespective of sexuality and family. We have, on the one hand, Islam, which subjugates women and fixes their servitude through the Text, and, on the other, the poet, who defines the feminine as desire and renewal. The feminine renews itself constantly and always. It is the infinite par excellence. The feminine is essentially against religion.

H: In order to evoke a self-renewing infinite, Ibn ʿArabī gives the floor to Bilqīs, just as Socrates allows Diotima, who is inside him, to speak.

A: Indeed. But ordinary men are on the side of religion, because religion goes hand in hand with power. And as the man is on the side of power, he wants to dominate femininity.

H: We constantly come back to this gap between the theological text and the mystical text. In the latter, the woman (Bilqīs) preaches the movement or calligraphy of the breath, while the man (Solomon) is in thrall to the desire for possession, power and triumph. Georges Bataille, who is considered to be the last mystic, said that the obelisk in Place de la Concorde should be demolished, as he saw it as a symbol of phallic possession.

A: I couldn't agree more. Like poetry, the feminine is essentially against religion. Poetry is the opposite of the religious spirit. Why? Because religion is a response. Poetry, on the other hand, is a question, and as such is at the opposite pole to power. In this sense, there is a great affinity between poetry and femininity. Islam has attacked both. It has transformed sexuality and Islamicized femininity. It has distorted its meaning by defining it as property, as a thing that can be possessed. The woman no longer belongs to herself. She has become the object of the man. Islam has separated masculinity and femininity in a quite radical way.

H: Even though we are all partly bisexual. Only, religion has placed masculinity on the side of power and femininity on the side of subjugation.

A: Worse. The masculine becomes the symbol of God. He is the king, the caliph on earth. And women are his property.

H: The Text says: 'Your wives are a tilth [*harth*] for you, so go into your tilth when you like.'[51]

A: And since she is *ḥarth* (tilth or field of labour), she exists only for reproduction. All her femininity, all her revolutionary dimension, all her beauty as an essential element of existence, of the cosmos, are meant to be eclipsed or disappear altogether.

H: Another verse says: 'and (as to) those on whose part you fear desertion, admonish them, and leave them alone in the sleeping-places and beat them'.[52] Not to mention *mā malakat al-yamīn*, literally 'that which the man possesses'. It is said: 'then marry such women as seem good to you, two and three and four [. . .] or what your right hands possess'.[53] I recall that 'marry' is a translation of the verb *inkaḥū*, which signifies 'take them' in the sexual sense. You could translate this as 'possess such women as seem good to you'.

A: And to reinforce this male superiority, religion has made woman the symbol of sin.

H: It's been that way since the Old Testament. Islam didn't introduce it, but it fell into step with the biblical text.

A: Islam followed and reinforced this trend. It transformed women into objects to be possessed and a code for sexuality. It thus instituted sexuality as law. From that point onwards we have had to deal with the licit and the illicit, in other words a codified object. It is the peak of the deformation and negation of the feminine, of women and of desire. Religion has deformed desire. It has deformed sexuality and love. I can even say that it has annulled love.

H: Nevertheless, in the Old Testament it is written that the man must leave his father and mother to follow his wife. We don't find this sort of statement in the Qur'an.

A: I'll qualify what I said: Islam has deformed sexuality, has denied love and deformed the relationship between the feminine self and the masculine other. It has deformed all relationships. The only one left is the one between master and slave, the one who possesses and the object possessed. In fact, Muslims have not paid attention to the fact that this mentality has killed even religion, because it has transformed it into a means which justifies possession and annuls spirituality. We had to go to the mystics to talk about spirituality.

H: Before Freud, the mystics talked about a psychic bisexuality. Each human being has two attributes. But what actually happened was terribly poignant. We went from Sumerian or Greek goddesses to women who become properties or shadows or ghosts. It is as if Islam was reinforcing the phallicity propounded by the Bible, as if it was created purely to strangle women.

A: It transforms the very personhood of women. When we say 'the woman in Islam', we automatically think of her sexual organs. Woman is a vagina. Islam has killed woman. There is no more woman, only a sexual organ or a ghost called 'the woman'. It has made her an instrument for the desire and pleasure of man. And it has used nature to establish and further consolidate its domination and power.

H: More virility for men and more servitude for women. To discuss, question or want to change necessarily entails blasphemy.

A: And you can't approach women on earth except via the code and the Law. I'll even go further: Islam, from this point of view, is an *istibāḥa*.

H: *Istibāḥa* means 'licentiousness'.

A: Licentiousness in the name of religion. One, two and three and four . . . or what your right hands possess. Historically and religiously, Islam has always encouraged conquests and *sabī* (taking prisoners).

H: Today, in the twenty-first century, there are women prisoners in cages up for sale. Islamic State fixes the price. The youngest, the small girls, are the most expensive. It's disgusting!

A: It is indeed disgusting. But it is essentially religious. The youngest are the most expensive because they are virgins. I've being saying this for a long time: Muslims are perpetually haunted by love and money. By money as power. You said, in the twenty-first century. Yes, but for Islamic State notions of man and human dignity do not exist.

H: The images are awful. Women in cages, dressed in white to signify that they are now Sunnis. I measure the progress of a society by the way it deals with the question of women. Contemporary Arab-Muslim society is outside of history.

A: Women before Islam were free, certainly freer than the woman under Islam.

H: Even the feminine side of men is condemned.

A: The feminine is banished. All that's left is the love of possession and a pleasure with *houris* fed by Qur'anic verses. In fact, it's not a question of women, but rather of these other creatures who exclusively incarnate sexuality. Women exist on earth. But Islam nurtures an exceptional imaginary by calling up something even more extraordinary: the *houri*. The concept of paradise is based on this pleasure without limits which is very different. Heaven, like earth, is founded on sexuality.

H: The Text gave four women to each man. But the Prophet, aside from his nine wives, had the right to concubines, their number unlimited by the Qur'an. The verse says: 'two and three and four [women]'. Heaven then becomes an extension of the pleasure men first experience on earth.

A: It is opened up to infinity. The man in Islam is a libertine. Religion gives him absolute freedom in the possession of women here on earth and in paradise. There is no restriction, no limit on pleasure.

H: We are seeing more and more Islamist videos popping up on YouTube. There is one of an imam saying that a man who, on his way home from work, sees a 'tempting' woman should return home and discharge his libido with his own woman. The Muslim woman should not go out to work but should remain at home and be available for her husband's need for discharge.

A: The worst thing is that Arab and Muslim revolutionaries cease to be revolutionaries once the woman question is dangled in front of them. Then revolutionaries become like fundamentalists.

H: I recall that it was the woman question which led you to shut down the review *Mawāqif*.

A: That's right. The editorial committee wanted to devote an issue of the review to the condition of women in the Arab world and in the Qur'anic text. They asked a specialist in Muslim law to write an article on the situation of women in light of the texts of law and jurisprudence. The specialist didn't dare write the article. I approached other jurists, who all refused to apply themselves to the brief. So I decided to close down the review.

H: Was this fear or the difficulty of confronting texts that were too unjust?

A: If you speak the truth you open yourself up to threats, judgement and persecution. In our countries, an individual who starts to reflect on this culture is taking his life in his hands. What I realized that day was that political and religious censorship had not desisted for fifteen centuries and that it was the very essence of our culture. I decided to not devote any more time to a review that was no longer able to defend the right to free speech and thought. I couldn't go on maintaining the lie of a revolt that lacked the courage to attack the essential problems of our everyday lives. So I decided to close down the review.

H: *Mawāqif* was a revolutionary review in the field of poetry, writing and politics. Its writers dared to attack the politics of Nasser when he was at the height of his powers. However, when it came to the matter of women, you could see the awkwardness and reticence. The subject has to remain taboo.

A: The religious foundation of the Arab man is alive and well.

H: Pierre Bourdieu, in a conversation with Günter Grass, expressed regret that intellectuals 'don't open their mouths more'. How can we account for the fact that these images of humiliated, terrorized, murdered women haven't provoked an uprising in the Arab world?

A: Muslims are like this in one form or another because they are born into a culture and a religion which have always belittled women. It is the Muslim unconscious. Women are not human beings but objects to buy and sell. So putting women in cages, selling them, determining their price on the basis of their age or their looks . . . this is all part of the history of Arab women. This is not new. Women in Islam are more objects than real human beings.

H: Apart from the disconcerting strangeness of the female sex, I think the reason our intellectuals don't protest is that religion has accorded so many privileges to men. When you talked about revolutionaries who deep down are still fundamentalists, that is something I have frequently come across to my personal cost when taking part in conferences and talking on the subject of women.

A: It's a sad phenomenon. The Arab man does not inhabit his earth. He is not in his own history. He is neither in Europe nor in Asia, nor in Oceania. He lives in heaven. All Muslim Arabs live in heaven. You might say that they have nothing to do with earth or history.

H: In Tunisia, the conservatives have taken advantage of the general confusion to reverse everything that Bourguiba tried to put in place, in other words, equality. But I do recall that Bourguiba nonetheless tried to create equality in everything except inheritance laws.

A: In fact the Qur'an says: 'The male shall have the equal of the portion of two females.'[54] Bourguiba made a considerable effort to try to install a secular culture. Let us not forget that equality and democracy do not emanate from the Qur'anic text or from Arab history. Democracy comes from the West. Today we talk about freedom. But freedom is a notion that doesn't exist in the Text or in the Islamic context. Freedom, and democracy, are notions that were created in the West; they were forged by Western thought.

H: Women were the biggest losers in the Arab Spring.

A: Women hadn't gained so much before that we can see them as losers today. Bourguiba attempted a separation of state and religion which was beneficial for women. In the Middle East, women were also able to make interesting advances in the fields of work, emancipation and family life . . . But our problem derives from the founding text, which governs socio-economic life in the Arab world. We expected the situation of women to evolve, if only because they were working and participating fully in the social and economic life of their country. Unfortunately, we have had to admit, with some bitterness, that their situation has got worse. In the past they may well have had a marginalized position, but they were also poets, musicians, dancers . . . they had a space in which they could excel. Today, Daesh, in Iraq and in Syria, runs contests to find the best reader of the Qur'an and offers a captive woman to the winner as a prize. It's a humiliation for women and the Holy Book.

H: It is especially humiliating for all women. I am starting to get a better grasp of your reflections concerning the un-changeability of the religious mentality in our countries. In Tunisia, secularism has borne fruit. But I've recently learned that Tunisian men are preferring to marry Algerian women or women from other Arab countries, because Tunisian women are too 'demanding' after having got used to the privileges instituted by Bourguiba.

A: The Arab man is still in a general sense fundamentally a religious being. That is a sad fact.

H: Reading the works of Antoinette Fouque, where she tackles questions of sexism, misogyny and machismo, I realized that these terms don't exist in Arabic. There are no Arabic terms for this mistreatment of women.

A: Contrary to Western society, nothing to do with sexuality or the sexual in Arab society has undergone any sort of cultural evolution. Women have never been regarded as beings possessing free will or the capacity to act or think; they have never been seen as autonomous beings who can contribute to the progress of society. Women are still dominated by masculine culture. And religion has reinforced this vision. It has even justified it theoretically. The Qur'an says: 'Men are the maintainers of women because Allah has made some of them to excel others.'[55]

H: It also says: 'and the men are a degree above them, and Allah is All-Mighty, Wise'.[56] And men repeat what the Qur'an says. In order to think about this injustice done to women, language in the West has invented words. This invention of words points to a social evolution. There is nothing like this in the Arabic language of today.

A: Right up to the present day, the common view is that the man gives and the woman receives. He is active, she is passive. However, in poetry, another image of women predominates: that of Fāṭima, Khawla, Maïa.[57] Whether it's a case of so-called profane, courtly or mystical poetry, woman occupies a place quite different from that attributed by the Qur'an. But in reply to your remark, to my knowledge there are no words in modern Arabic to express: sexism, machismo, misogyny. I repeat: the woman is seen as passive in life as in sexuality. Voluptuousness belongs to the masculine. The woman must be content with being the place of pleasure for him.

H: While working on ancient Arabic texts, I found this expression, which I didn't understand and which you explained to me: 'She was *taḥta fulān*', she was under so-and-so; in other words: she was his wife.

A: This expression does not simply designate the woman as a passive being, it also speaks volumes about the contempt for women. She is literally under someone. This bodily position signifies domination. She has no choice but to be dominated or possessed.

H: The Arabic language has not evolved. The term *ʿadhrā* (virgin) is only used in the feminine. As if man was not the fruit of a history and a journey. He is born a man. He doesn't become one.

A: This shows that society has not evolved. The woman has to be the place where the man can realize whatever he wants and realize himself through her. Consequently, she is nothing but a means for the satisfaction of the man/the masculine/the active. I would add that the absence of nature and the religious formatting had the effect that psychoanalytical thinking had difficulty taking root in Arab culture. Especially when it was a question of the veil or of women. Moreover, the figure of woman-nature is absent. She has been replaced by the woman commanded by the Text (the woman-*shar*').

Woman has disappeared, reduced to a womb, and femininity is no more than a tilth or field of labour for man.

H: Our society regards motherhood as the sole destiny of a woman. The menopause is known in Arabic as *sinnu l'ya's* (the time of despair). The woman has nothing else to do but mope around until she dies.

A: It is an extreme injustice towards women and everything relating to them. Nature, instead of being an enigma or a mystery, has become, like woman herself, a landscape created by God for the pleasure of the faithful. Truth, from the Islamic point of view, is in the hands of God. It resides in the text and not in the reality of experience. Consequently, the spirit is condemned the moment it expresses a desire to understand the mystery of the transformations of the universe. Knowledge was limited in the Revelation. And life became a simple bridge to paradise or the other world preached by the holy word. It is this legend of Revelation-language that commands the world or existence.

H: Reflecting on the veil as a cloth covering the body of the woman prevents us from taking up again those very beautiful mystical texts which define the word as the veil of things. The veil is reduced to an impoverished, even vulgar meaning that contrasts with the reflection of the mystics or that very subtle reading by Jacques Derrida and Hélène Cixous, for example, in *Veils*.

A: Femininity has been superseded by the single womb. It has become a field to be cultivated. According to Sophocles, time unveils truths; from the Islamic point of view, these are unveiled only by God.

H: In Morocco, women are starting to join groups that denounce marital rape. Women are becoming conscious that they are sometimes the locus of the realization of their husbands' wildest fantasies. Nevertheless, there is still no judicial term in Arabic to designate marital rape. That is, in order to denounce marital rape, sexism, machismo . . . you have to resort to a Western language. Our beautiful language remains impoverished when it comes to thinking about male–female relations at the heart of society today. Is it possible for me to put it in these terms?

A: Yes, you can. However, we should make it clear that this is to do not so much with the weakness of the language as with the absence of reflection and innovation in Arab culture. According to the Text, the poet, the writer, the thinker had no free self to freely express their subjectivity. They found it difficult to express their thoughts on the subject of woman, sexuality, the body . . . Absence of freedom means absence of subjectivity and a difficulty in adapting to social transformations. How can an individual deprived of his self and his liberty think? That's the issue I tried to raise in the text you mentioned earlier on the absence of subjectivity in Salafi culture.

H: But at the same time, I find that it is one of the greatest paradoxes of the Arab world. Contrary to the mystical literature or philosophical thought, which started and ended in a particular historical period, erotic literature has spanned the centuries.

A: As long as we make clear that there are many Arab erotic texts, but women in them are little more than puppets. There are a large number of works on sexuality: How do you possess women? How can men be gods to women? How do you give her an orgasm? Etc. They are all centred on men's virility and their sexual prowess. The woman is described as the one who must open herself to this virility. She is simply putty in the hands of men.

H: So you are saying that even erotic texts have not liberated women from the possession advocated by the Qur'anic text and the hagiographers.

A: There are in fact two discourses. One is linked to the Qur'an, hence to religion. It is the official discourse that still predominates in the Arab world. Then there is another, marginalized discourse, which comes from the pre-Islamic world and pre-Islamic poetry, which celebrates another type of life in Arab society: one where women have a status and other conditions of life. For example, when 'Imru'u l-Qays says: 'Behind her, if his [the child's] tears flowed, she offered him her breast / While under me was offered her lower belly.'[58]

H: She is a mother and fully a woman. So this is not the usual split between mother and woman.

A: Many poets depict a magnificent image of the woman. She might be a goddess, the Lady, someone who can choose to say yes or no to men ... So we must bear in mind the existence of these two discourses: the religious discourse, which goes against the human and condemns women, and the other, non-religious discourse, which is subterranean and marginalized, of course, but which is more human. Magnificently human.

H: And there is a mystical discourse . . .

A: . . . which has saved poetry and thought and has celebrated the feminine. It is fortunate that we have poetry to embody the love of the feminine and poets whose vision exceeds the narrowness of the religious vision. The mystic says: 'Any place that does not feminize itself is sterile.'[59]

H: Masculine and feminine, in mysticism as much as in psychoanalysis, are not tributaries of anatomy. If the woman poses any real problem to man in all societies, and particularly in ours, it is that she calls into question his relationship with castration.

A: The Arab male refuses the idea of castration. He thinks of himself and sees himself as all-powerful.

H: Castration is a difficult concept in our societies, and language has not evolved enough to be open to social transformations. How do we create a modernity?

A: Possibly the terms have had difficulty seeing the light of day because of religious censorship. We should pay attention to what is happening today. Instead of talking about women's freedom, their rights, how to improve the conditions of their lives, etc., the Islamic State and the self-styled modern Arab revolutionaries have created a greater subjugation for women and more pleasure for men.

H: The supposed Arab revolution has lifted the veil on this extremely primitive relationship between men and women in Arab society. A book entitled *As'adu imra'a fi-l-'ālam* (*The Happiest Woman in the World*), written by a Saudi Wahhabi, is the book most frequently purchased today. The happiest woman is the one who shows the greatest submission to the precepts and consequently to her husband.

A: This extremely archaic relationship comes from the primitive side of Islam and the religious division of the sexes and of sexuality.

H: Not many people know that the Wahhabi state destroyed the house of Fāṭima[60] in 2006, seeing it as a vestige of female rebellion.

A: And that of 'Ā'isha. I repeat: the relationship of religion to women is radically different from that of the poet. Poets have always been bards of the woman and of femininity. The poet al-'Arjī[61] says: 'What use to me is Mina and its pilgrims / If she is not there.' The holy place has no value unless it includes the beloved. And Mecca, the sacred place, becomes secondary to the vision of the woman. That is one of the reasons why religion condemns poetry. Contrary to the poet, who makes himself a bard of the woman, the theologians demand that she be veiled.

H: As if the unveiling and autonomy of the woman were the supreme threat to men. The threat of castration. Even her voice is prohibited, according to some commentators on the Text cited by Tabarī. She should remain hidden, as if she must perforce be a Baubo, and each face was a sex. And when Tabarī interprets the verse 'Beat them', he writes that man can possess her without saying a word to her. Thus, he can rape her. The rape of women as a form of punishment appears in a book that acts as an authority on the religious sciences.

A: It should be said that, beyond the woman question, in Arab society the individual cannot dialogue freely with a different other. Speech is not adopted, democratic dialogue and the exchange of opinions are not accepted. Violence alone predominates. In this climate, a woman who liberates herself is a woman who contests and openly expresses her disagreement. But that is not allowed.

H: In the West they use the word *burqa* to describe the full-length veil. But this word indicates a veiling not of the feminine being of the woman, but of her very humanity, because *burqa* means 'ewe' or the 'crawling animal' or 'beast of burden'. The word was used to refer to Bedouin women who worked in the fields like beasts of burden.

A: It is a terrible and humiliating image of country women.

H: There is a forgetfulness of history here too. Remember the militancy of Algerian women in gaining independence for their country.

A: They haven't received the recognition they deserved. In any case, in the other Arab countries, none of the progressive women of the twentieth century, such as May Ziade,[62] Huda Sha'rawi[63] and many others, were recognized in the movement of social liberation. Qāsim Amīn[64] is discussed more than Huda Sha'rawi. The most militant woman is marginalized and her texts are not taught. Only men are talked about, even when it is about women. Yet there were female writers, actors, singers ... The West abounds with great women. We have forgotten ours.

H: May Ziade had a literary salon. But she came up against the masculine imaginary opposed to learned women.

A: The West is ignorant of these great literary figures, who are relatively unknown in the East too. May Ziade founded what was essentially a literary salon which was attended by Taha Hussein, al-'Aqqād, al-Māzinī ... and other major men of letters from the beginning of the twentieth century. This was extraordinary for the time. But her family, who disapproved of her, accused her of being mad. However, the writer Antoun Sa'āde defended her and wrote many fine things about her and her writing. In fact, despite the censure and the weight of tradition, there were some highly engaged women in Lebanon, Egypt, Syria, Iraq and Palestine. Algerian women such as Djamila Bouhired fought hard for the independence of their country. But they were victims of the archaic mentality that continues to reign to this day.

H: Certain female novelists and essayists took pseudonyms so as not to reveal their patronyms, such as Samira

'Bint al-Jazīra al-'Arabiya' and 'Ā'isha 'Bint ash-Shāti',[65] as if the learned woman were some sort of curse.

A: They took these pseudonyms out of fear and to counteract patriarchal power. They knew that they were part of a society where the woman could not express herself freely. In the eyes of men she had to remain as one who did not think.

H: Nevertheless, it is often said that women, especially mothers, are the greatest guardians of our tradition.

A: I personally think that it is about religion, not tradition. The woman is the man's possession. And the fact that girls are meant to remain virgins until their wedding day signifies that they are still the object of men. Don't forget that there is a verse on the subject of virginity. The Qur'an says: 'Surely We have made them to grow into a (new) growth, / Then We have made them virgins.'[66]

H: I think it is also about a history of pleasure. Often, women are repudiated when it is discovered that their girls have 'lost their virginity'. The mother, a woman living in a traditional context where sexuality is codified, when she is repudiated, finds herself without a man and thus without the possibility of enjoying sexual relations. The girl's pleasure outside of marriage can lead to the abolition of pleasure for her mother.

A: There is indeed this psychological aspect. But female pleasure remains a big taboo subject. It isn't talked about. Only male sexuality has any importance. In our society, man has replaced God. And the Muslims imitate Muhammad. The mentality of the Muslim and Arab man remains profoundly religious. His mental and psychic structure is religious. He is marked with domination, power and influence. The woman finds herself caught in this mechanism without any real escape or exit.

H: Daesh has closed down the power of interpretation (*ijtihād*) which was inaugurated by the caliph 'Umar.

A: As I have already said, the absence of self and subjectivity has left no space for free thought. The Arab is trying to create his modernity without recourse to it. He lives in a society that produces more clerics than intellectuals. He is born and grows up in a culture that suffers from the absence of freedom. Freedom remains the exclusive property of those who exercise power. A power that pursues the feminine. In the past, women were discredited. Today, women are captives offered up as gifts. It is humiliating! I would add: any society that believes that it is in possession of the absolute truth produces ignorance. This ignorance not only takes the place of science and knowledge, it actually turns into a perpetual revolt against science and knowledge. Monotheism is a distortion of culture. It needs to be torn up, not reformed.

H: Through this humiliation of the woman, what hatred for the sister, the cousin, the wife . . . It is also a way for the man to crush the traces of femininity inside him and perhaps to crush a problematic love for his sister. And even today a woman who has been raped says to her husband: *hatakūlak* '*arḍak* (They have violated your honour). It is not about her body or her psyche, but rather the honour ('*arḍ*) of the man.

A: '*Arḍ* is seen as a sign of the masculine. *Al-'Arḍ* is the feminine form of the masculine, sexually speaking. We don't say *hataka 'arḍahā* (he has violated her honour), as she doesn't exist in her own right. She has no thoughts, no personality, no feelings and no body to belong to her. She is and remains connected to him. Consequently, the problem remains that of the man: he is the one who is humiliated, not her. The Arab man lives in a space that has undergone cultural and technological transformations. He lives in a context that is radically different from the past but he continues to believe in a problematic manner. Is that a strength or a weakness?

H: In psychoanalysis this is known as the 'split self'. It is a defence mechanism which reveals a certain strength – albeit pathological – and a weakness, because the individual can't face the trauma that is: the basic drives of the foundation of Islam. So the split subject bases his identity on the cohabitation inside him of this strength and this weakness.

A: So he is like a container full of verses. In a general manner, he is fashioned like a robot or a machine. I ponder over the nature of the link between *āla* (machine) and *ilāh* (divinity). It is almost the same word and the same letters make up the two terms. Is this a linguistic accident?

H: There was an Arabian goddess called Allāt. They took two diacriticals from the name to make the Allāh of Muslim monotheism. Might we then say: since they took away the marks of femininity, has the divine become an *āla*, a machine?[67]

A: Today, there is nothing left of religion but a machine of extermination. Daesh represents this transformation of the divine into a machine that exterminates.

H: It's a triumph over the feminine. But the world can't exist without femininity.

A: Man without femininity and without this dimension of the feminine becomes a machine. We have already mentioned the words of Ibn 'Arabī: '*Kullu makānin lā yu'annath, lā yu'awwal 'alayh*' (Any place that does not accept the feminine doesn't count [is sterile, vain]). I would extend this further: 'Any place commanded by a singular virility, *lā yu'awwal 'alayh*, is sterile.' Having said this, women continue to fight against this virile mentality. I have noticed that young people in the Arab countries have a strong desire to change things and have done with this archaism. Young people today are more aware of the threat that weighs down on the present and the future.

H: What is your opinion of FEMEN?[68]

A: I'm not against them. Especially in the type of society that categorically denies them. But I hope that society will recognize femininity as it recognizes masculinity.

H: Antoinette Fouque says: soon there will be no one but the old, soon there will be no more Blacks and Whites, just coffee-coloureds. But women will always remain women. That is, with this load of injustices weighing down on them.

A: We clearly need a separation of state and religion. The creation of a civil society is a necessity. We shouldn't be talking about Muslims but citizens, about their rights and their freedom. The biggest enemy of woman isn't men, it is religion. Especially monotheist religion, primarily Islam.

H: It is a scandal that in this day and age, in certain Gulf States, an educated woman can't vote whereas an illiterate man can. Women have been deprived of the right to vote, hence to express themselves. Yet according to the Constitution, 'every human being, of whatever sex, irrespective of race, religion or belief, possesses inalienable and sacred rights'.

A: It's against the very idea of the human and of progress. I even wonder how men can accept this. The error was in concentrating on the regimes and forgetting that a revolution requires the human being to change, and that this change must be real and radical. There has to be an internal revolt in the name of freedom, for freedom, for thought and democratic dialogue with the other. We have to accept the other in his difference. This is not possible unless based on the creation of a secular society. I deplore this regression. We have been fighting for the last two centuries to create a secular civil society and we now find ourselves face to face with a scandalous obscurantism that is in the process of exterminating the first stirrings of modernity.

Beyond Economic and Geopolitical Interests: The Drives

H: We hear more and more about radicalization.

A: We can't understand this phenomenon unless we take the time to reconsider the birth of Islam. As we have said, violence was intrinsically linked to the birth of Islam. It was born as a form of power. And this violence accompanied the foundation of the first caliphate and draws from certain Qur'anic verses and the first commentaries on the Text.

H: Daesh takes us back to this time when people had to convert to Islam or die.

A: We have mentioned a number of verses. But the Qur'an contains many others that are extremely violent. This violence has become institutionalized. It is now part of the state institution. Let us also mention that, from the start, Muslims were conquerors. The century following the death of Muhammad was bloody, and the Arab–Arab and Muslim–Muslim wars never ceased. You just have to read the works on the history of the Arabs.

H: But why did Islam resist the transformation?

A: We didn't take human nature into account, or at least not sufficiently: power, money and violence. Islam awoke in people the instinct for possession.

H: That is: we didn't refer to the psychological dimension and speak about the drives in our search for answers. The foundational text and the first commentaries in effect allowed men to fully satisfy their drives, in particular the drive for mastery and the sexual drive. The idea of a paradise as the place of total satisfaction where the notion of want ceases to exist derives from a fantasy or from a denial of castration. The foundation grasped something of the nature of the drive and fantasy. Can we talk about a sickness of Islam, as did 'Abd'el-Wahāb Meddeb?

A: In *The Sickness of Islam*, Meddeb also talks about a fine and true Islam.

H: But within this Muslim universe there is mysticism, philosophy, literature . . .

A: These intellectual movements do not arise from Islam as a state or institution. The mystics and the philosophers used Islam as a veil or as a means of escaping persecution and executions. Philosophy does not emanate from the Qur'anic text.

H: Indeed, it comes from Greece, and mysticism has drawn upon different currents: Platonism, neo-Platonism, Christianity, language . . . But those who forged this thought lived at the heart of Muslim society.

A: The mystics of Islam quoted from the Text to justify their interpretations. But, reading their works, we see a large discrepancy with the Qur'anic text. Ibn 'Arabī, for example, forged a system of thought that broke radically with the religious and Muslim conception of man and the universe.

H: Ibn 'Arabī was a great philologist. His concern wasn't the precept, but what language hid in its semantic cores. Like you, he was a lover of the language. His thought hinged on what language could express and the reality that it couldn't say.

A: He was a poet and had no connection with doctrine, dogma or religious thought. His writings, like the words of al-Ḥallāj, had nothing to do with orthodox thinking or religious education. It was a strategy or a sort of defence. It is what we are doing now: we are looking for a great and true Islam in order to protect ourselves from violence. One might even say that Ibn 'Arabī liberated the language of Islam. The thinkers in Arab society were obliged to borrow a mask called 'Islam' in order to get around the order to kill any Muslim who abandoned his religion. Those who didn't, such as al-Ḥallāj, faced persecution and death sentences, not to mention the destruction of their work. Niffarī, for example, wrote a book which wasn't rediscovered for another thousand years. It remains unrecognized.

H: Even when the book is published, the thinker remains unrecognized. A fatwa in Egypt opposed the republication of the *Futūḥāt al-makkiyya* of Ibn 'Arabī, edited for the first time by the emir 'Abd el-Qāder. This being so, I think that

Averroes, Abū Bakr al-Rāzī, Ibn al-Rāwandī, Niffarī ... are all part of Arab society, as dissidents.

A: Mysticism and philosophy are not part of Islamic thought, which is nothing more than *fiqh* (jurisprudence) and *shar'* (Law).

H: Since we have talked about al-Ḥallāj, I would like to recall these magnificent words: when Satan refused to prostrate himself before Adam, saying that he could not change the object of his love, God said to him: 'I will torture you for ever', and Satan responded: 'Won't you look at me?' 'I will', said God. 'Then your gaze will lift me beyond torture. Do with me as you wish.' Al-Ḥallāj will be damned by love. And this exchange between love and the divine summons up a whole reflection on the language of mysticism, love, transgression and femininity.

A: We see that femininity, like the feminine, goes beyond woman. It is a position. And divinity is a state and a position also. Femininity is the universe itself. It is not the imaginary of official Islam. Mysticism expressed love of the feminine and of the woman. It overturned thinking about the question of alterity and subjectivity. Yet in the Text subjectivity does not exist.

H: In a television programme, you said that the dialogue between God and Satan was very democratic. They disagreed, but they talked. God could have exterminated him on the spot, but he let him express himself.

A: Today we don't have that possibility any more. Muslims don't even respect their Text. Dialogue is not permitted. The believer thinks that he possesses the absolute truth. At this point, according to him, all other beliefs are false and must be rejected. This sort of belief has transformed Islamic politics into a *techne*, the ultimate purpose of which is power and how to retain it. The whole of Arab history attests to this fact. Their culture is a culture of power. Today, politically and economically, Arabs can buy the world, thanks to their oil and gas. However, they possess neither Averroes nor Ibn Khaldūn nor al-Ma'arrī.

H: I remember a conference in Oran on mysticism. In vain I searched through *Mawāqif* (*The Book of Haltings*) of the emir 'Abd el-Qāder, who was a major commentator on Ibn 'Arabī.

A: In this sense the Arabs are the poorest of the poor. They know neither their own culture nor their own language. How can they make a revolution? On what basis, on what underlying principles?

H: Daesh advocates an Islamic State. But this runs counter to every idea of civilization. In *Civilization and Its Discontents*, Freud says that civilization can't be built except by renouncing satisfaction of the basic drives. But what do we find? Possession of women, disembowelling, beheadings and even cannibalism . . .

A: The man who thinks that he is stronger than death – because he will have a place in paradise – can practise acts of barbarism without fear or a sense of guilt. He is separated from nature and from culture. I see in Daesh the end of Islam. A prolongation too, of course. But the end all the same. Without the fervour or vision to change the world, no thought, no art, no science. This repetition is the very marker of its end. Even supposing Daesh achieved victory on a political or strategic level, what could it offer on the intellectual or scientific level?

H: Apart from chaos, I can't see anything. In the areas already conquered by Islamic State in Iraq, schools have been suspended pending a new education programme in line with the tenets of religion.

A: Daesh is not a new reading of Islam, nor the construction of a new culture or a new civilization. Rather, it is closure, ignorance, hatred of knowledge, hatred of the human and of freedom. And it is a humiliating end. Historically speaking, Islam has lived for fifteen centuries. Compared to the whole history of humanity, that is a short time: it will have lasted less time than the pharaohs, the Greeks, the Romans ... There is a real sickness here, because a religion that has a vision and a plan can't give itself permission to cut people's throats. And instead of championing freedom, today it reinforces servitude. The individual who lives in Arab society suffers from the absence of freedom: freedom of expression, freedom of belief, freedom of writing, equality between men and women. Up until now, civil and secular society has not managed to exist. The notion of secularity remains banned. Political power lies beyond freedom. And when a struggle is linked not to progress but to power, these revolutions free people from one prison only to lead them into another.

H: It is true that we have adopted the habit of conducting economic, socio-political and strategic analyses. But we haven't taken the time to reflect on the psychological dimension. Looking at what is happening today, it's hard not to think in terms of the death drive or the drive to destruction. Because it is a form of self-destruction. When they destroy all vestiges and traces, the fanatics are wiping out their own history and exterminating the peoples who belong to their lands, their brothers and sisters. We need to look at this phenomenon in the light of psychoanalytical texts on the drives, parricide, matricide, fratricide, castration and pleasure.

A: Wahhabism is in the process of exterminating all traces of the human. Once you posit that God is the author of all works, humans cannot invent, create or realize visual, musical or poetic works . . . and where you have a single Creator, you have to erase all human creation. For it is *wathan* (idol). It derives from idolatry. This explains the destruction of museums and archaeological sites. They destroy any work by human beings because it is assumed to be a challenge to God. Man is supposed to be nothing more than an executor of the precepts. God creates and man imitates.

H: The following verse comes to mind: 'So you did not throw when you threw, but it was Allah Who threw.'[1] Our memory is fashioned by phrases that we never interrogate . . .

A: And when it is He who throws and does everything else, the human has no function other than to be commanded or remote controlled. So all traces of human creation must be erased, even just the throwing of a simple object, a pebble for example, does not come from an individual human decision but is dictated by God, who decides everything. In this context the human finds it difficult to raise itself to the noble heights of creativity because it has to tackle the religious interdict and the common and widespread perception that any spirit of initiative is an attack against the divine. The Qur'anic verse speaks of the erasure of the human and of the traces of his passage on earth. '*Wa yabqā wajhu rabbika*' ('And there will endure forever the person of your Lord, the Lord of glory and honour').[2] Can we build a civilization while exterminating man and that which is profoundly human?

H: Current events clearly reveal that what is intended is far from the very idea of culture. They show instead evidence of the triumph of the drives.

A: It is not the sickness of Islam, but rather of culture, of the civility of the human. I would add: it is a self-loathing that leads as far as suicide. In order to find paradise, thousands of people are ready to go and blow themselves up. This phenomenon is unique in the entire history of civilization. It's a first in the entire history of humanity. The aforementioned jihadists find eternal pleasure – that of the paradise described by the Qur'an. If pleasure on earth is ephemeral, that in the hereafter is eternal, absolute. The Islamic vision, by recourse to an image of paradise with its cohorts of *houris*, has transformed sex into a tool of seduction for belief. The Muslim who dies a Muslim or who dies for Islam doesn't die, he simply absents himself from earth to dwell in paradise next to God. And in this paradise, he has multiple possibilities of pleasure.

H: Vladimir Bartol, in *Alamut*, imagined this scenario: young fanatics kill themselves to find paradise, which is synonymous in their minds with women and pleasure. It's the question of pleasure that constantly crops up.

A: The erotic thus takes on a divine dimension. Man has invented the image of a phallus in paradise which remains as erect as an *alif*, destined to penetrate women, in order to reinforce the idea that the latter are nothing but objects of possession over which he can exercise his power as conqueror. Thus, even in the hereafter, the woman remains the one penetrated, the one possessed. The phallus becomes a sort of natural *fascinum* which never stops and thus is the symbol of power and authority.

H: The Wahhabi imams on YouTube preach only about eternal pleasure. There is even an imam who used the theory of relativity to explain that, instead of the forty or seventy women promised, each Muslim will have, in the hereafter, seventy who will each have seventy slave women to offer to the man each day, in the knowledge that a day in the hereafter is longer than a day here on earth. Male pleasure is without end. No limits means no castration. What is happening now leads us to reflect on the connection between the first commentators on the Text and the question of castration.

A: What is happening today merits a psychoanalytical study. The man and woman of the jihad are depicted as sharing pleasure within a rite that elevates them. Each of them rises up towards that which is beyond them. They cease to be individuals forming part of a human society after this consummation or coupling to become universal beings.

H: At the same time, being in pleasure before encountering death, tasting absolute and indescribable pleasure is a way of tasting incest. On the psychic level, it is a regression. And if we look closely at Daesh's black flag, we notice the absence of diacriticals. Even writing is expected to regress.

A: It's a general regression. And those who try to find another Islam in the heart of Islam never succeed. Dominant Islam does not recognize anything that contradicts it. We have evoked the war declared against philosophers, mystics and poets. What is missing there is the recognition of the other as different. Islam refuses and bans anything that contradicts its theses: this shows a great intolerance. It doesn't recognize the equality between individuals or human beings. I might add that it doesn't advocate progress, because our present is the future-past.

H: Every intellectual movement comes up against the politico-religious. So we need to approach the religious text in a secular manner. Only a secular approach will guarantee a free interpretation and reading of our corpus.

A: And we have to invent a new form of reading that profoundly and essentially distinguishes between individual religious practice and the collective and social dimension. Without this new, modern reading Islam will remain a prisoner of violence and political power. We require a new form of reading that separates the political, cultural and social from each person's religious belief. Religion should be an individual question. How can Islam, which accepts that Jews or Christians might abandon their religion to convert to Islam, refuse to accept that someone who was born a Muslim might choose another religion?

H: In your opinion, we can't ever talk about multiple Islams?

A: There isn't a moderate Islam and an extremist Islam, a true Islam and a false Islam. There is one Islam. On the other hand, we have the possibility of other readings.

H: We have the *fuqahā'* (theologians) who nurture Wahhabism and thus Sharia, and those informed by Greek or Western philosophy, the human sciences . . . which can no longer accept this first Islam. There are those who advocate suppressing embarrassing verses. Is this a solution? Either it is a divine text and we make do with that, which seems a tall order in the twenty-first century, or we invent our own modernity. In fact, from the start, we have been interrogating the underlying drives and symbols of our identity.

A: We need a new reading: a free and considered one. And we have to escape this amalgam between Islam and Identity. Religion is not an identity. And I recall these two facts: At the time of the Islamic conquests, the world was virtually empty.

The new religion didn't have a large civilization to face ...
So Islam was able to prevail. But today it finds itself face to
face with a civilization which has made a radical break with
the past. It hasn't been able to dialogue with the advances
of modern civilization. As such, Islam belongs to the past.
Thus, historically speaking, it is finished.

H: Anthropologists are interested in religion because their
interest is focused on the symbolic bases of culture. When
you say 'it is finished', I understand this as: this excess of the
drives has sounded the death knell of a religion based more
on the drives than on symbols. It is awful.

A: Awful indeed. When you look at Islam in the world
today, you feel overcome with bitterness and anger, and you
want to rise up against it. Ignorance, cruelty, obscurantism
... slitting the throats of women, disembowelling them,
rape, pillage ... These are signs of the death of the human.
And Muslims themselves say nothing about this reality. The
occasional, isolated voice of protest, no more. But there is no
real opposition.

H: As well as fear, conditioning or education, this is perhaps due to a sideration or paralysis preventing reaction or
thought.

A: It is shameful, whatever the case.

H: A renaissance needs a period of latency, and this is true
of a fall also. What we are experiencing now may well be the
agony of a world.

A: And this agony will be a long one. I say that with regret: my father, who was a Muslim, initiated me in religion and poetry.

H: You wrote a text on the lack of scientific progress within the Islamic conception of the world. But the human sciences have not really gained a foothold in the Arab intellectual scene. For example, demons are projections. But to say this constitutes blasphemy, because their existence is attested by the Qur'anic text. There are psychotics who talk about jinns, but society, steeped in religious education, supports their psychosis. We've hardly begun to talk properly about psychosis and neurosis in our societies.

A: Even today and even in universities, people continue to talk about a man marrying a she-devil or a woman marrying a genie.

H: In the first case it's about Bilqīs. In the Muslim version she becomes the wife of Solomon. Legend has it that she was half human, half she-devil. I would say: like every woman, so as not to become entangled in a literalist reading.

A: We might say that Islam is a very fertile subject matter for psychoanalysts like you. Magical thinking, legend and superstition dominate Muslim culture. Muslims are haunted by the legends, which are considered to be absolute truths. No place for scientific thinking.

H: Magical thinking, supported by religion and illiteracy, is a major impediment to psychoanalysis taking root in

Muslim soil. Psychoanalysis is an atheist mode of thought which penetrates to the depths of the human. These depths are the drives, psychic bisexuality, fantasy . . . In our culture we haven't yet reflected on the absence of parricide in Islam, on the question of that cleavage whereby the first transmitters wrote about terror with absolutely no experience of it . . .

A: Any psychoanalytical or philosophical knowledge which could open up horizons or indeed deconstruct legend is attacked. Islam is by definition anti-psychoanalytical, because psychoanalysis opens up new horizons for reflection and thought.

H: It can even usurp God.

A: Of course. Psychoanalysis, in its essence, breaks with religion.

H: In this context it is difficult for the Arab world to give birth to a Freud.

A: Freud wasn't a citizen of a Jewish country. He lived in Vienna. He was a European of Jewish origin. There are Jews whose thought is liberated from religion. But Islam, as I have already said, has from the moment it was born prevented all thought that might question it and question its founding principles. And the Arabs who come from Arab societies become French, American, Canadian or German, etc. Those who currently live in France, like you, like me, aren't strictly speaking part of Arab society or Muslim culture. What do you have to do with Arab culture, apart from the love you feel for your family?

H: Just a love of the language and the desire to transform history-as-legend into history-as-work, following the formula of Michel de Certeau.

A: Islam has limited even language. It has not allowed it free expression in all fields of knowledge. Our language today should be opening up to modernity.

H: I think it's a pity that people who don't read you in Arabic don't see the extent to which you deconstruct the Qur'anic text in *The Book of the Siege, Ismail* or *Al-Kitāb*. I say to myself that the Westerner who reads Adonis doesn't grasp the deconstruction and the a-religiosity of his work. Taking hold of a verse, you relate the rooting of legend and magical thinking in Muslim culture.

A: I wanted to deconstruct this religious culture, to relaunch thought and language. But if anyone asked me today: 'What can you offer as a Muslim?' I would say: 'I can't offer anything as a Muslim.'

H: You love Christ!

A: As I love Ibn 'Arabī, Niffarī, Abū Nuwās . . . As I love poetry and creativity. Christ was a poet.

The West:
Passionately, Madly

H: No uprising to protest against what is happening now. It's as if the intellectuals have deserted the political sphere.

A: Perhaps because culture has become more and more like a trade. And the intellectual has been transformed into a functionary, like a civil servant. And once he is a functionary, he stops wanting to change things. You can't be a functionary and produce creative thought. The generation of Sartre, Camus, Raymond Aron and others has left its imprint. Political engagement was added to intellectual engagement. Sartre's struggle was intellectual as well as political.

H: Globalization has perhaps trapped intellectuals and thought generally. There is now a single economy and a single culture.

A: In Europe, society has grown old. It is tired, exhausted even, especially by economic problems: everyone is looking for work. People are afraid of the future. There are almost four million people in France out of work. People are anxious and looking to protect themselves instead of opening up to the future. Consequently, we need something new so that European society can change and offer a cultural vision and project.

H: Bourdieu said: 'We need to revive utopias.'

A: Utopia could be one project. But in the Arab world, instead of creating a future, we are facing an absolute project: to espouse religion. Europe is starting to regress too, if only because Western politics in a general way upholds the obscurantism embodied by Wahhabism.

H: The West has always propped up dictators in the Arab world.

A: Yes, absolutely. The West is not seeking culture, light, the future, progress. It is seeking money.

H: I have often asked myself this question: how is that, instead of supporting the revolutionary movements in the Arab world, the West deals with the most reactionary regimes?

A: I would like to stress that, when we talk about the West, we are discussing the political institution, not individuals. The political institution has held on to a tradition of domination in its relationship with the Arab peoples. The political institution still holds on to memories of Poitiers and Andalusia. These memories remain vivid.

H: Don't you think that there is also a feeling of indebtedness vis-à-vis the Arabs who introduced Hellenic thought in the Middle Ages?

A: We should recall that the Arab philosophers were just a bridge. They were intermediaries and not creators. The only innovator was Averroes, the commentator on Aristotle, whose work was as powerful as it was subversive. He was banned in Europe, especially in France, as he was seen as a major subversive. Also, he was regarded as an enemy.

H: Others, such as Avicenna and Ibn al-Haytham, the Alhazen of the Latinists, helped to introduce the Greeks while creating a singular body of work. Ibn al-Haytham was the first in physics to talk about the nature of the *lumen*. His work was translated by Vitellion, a monk in Silesia, who never mentioned the author's name.

A: There were a few illustrious names, for sure. But the institutional West doesn't have the same attitude towards the Arabs as it does towards the Chinese or Japanese, for example. The collective memory of the West retains the memory of the Crusades and colonization. The colonial spirit is still alive and well.

H: There is also the religious aspect: relations with the Far East are different, because they are not monotheists.

A: Exactly. So the relationship between the West and the Arab world remains ambiguous and very complex. That is why the institutional West doesn't want to deal with the

Arabs except on the political and commercial level. The West is interested in the Arabs because of their wealth and their strategic importance – but not on the level of civilization. We should add that Islam is essentially anti-West. In fact, the institutional West deals with institutional Islam. And institutional Islam is politics and the economy in connection with oil and gas. The institutional West has nothing to do with the great Arab creators or with the aspirations of the Arab left, with the separation of state and religion. Today, the political West sustains the fundamentalists.

H: So the aspirations of Arabs and their left-wing movements are attacked by Wahhabism and by the West, which has always watched over the dictatorial regimes.

A: There are two gigantic forces arraigned against an Arab left. And let us not forget that Islam from 1258, i.e. since the fall of Baghdad, is nothing more than a regression. Even if it has taken on the hue of everything that is modern, it remains a prisoner of this regression.

H: But there were attempts in the nineteenth and early twentieth centuries, particularly in the field of writing. Writers called out for a deconstruction of the traditional vision of the world.

A: There were indeed attempts by the great names. But the traditional vision won out.

H: Should we attribute this to a lack of preparation? Of will? The illiteracy of the majority? Or lack of time?

A: All of the above combined. Nevertheless, there is a fundamental reason, I think: Arab societies embrace Muslims or believers who do not question their faith. Instead of daring, radical and thorough reflection on our traditions or culture, the intellectuals settled for superficial analysis. Moreover, all the secular movements failed. And the West equally worked to prevent the emergence of a genuine Arab left. Let's take the state of Yemen, for example. Aden was renowned for being part of a left-wing movement. The West saw this little state as a big enemy. This shows that the West doesn't want any change in the Arab world. It battles against a better future for these societies.

H: Is the Arab world the sick child of the West? That might be more accurate than the formula 'the sickness of Islam'.

A: The West treats Arabs as puppets or marionettes, not as masters of their own destiny.

H: So it's an old sick person. And the political West is determined to tend to this sick person. He is not allowed to die. But he is not allowed to live either.

A: The West prefers to deal with Arabs in very precise areas: politics, economics and power ... On the other hand, the fundaments of Islam, its vision, its view of the human and of the world, are of no interest to the Western political institution. The West is taking advantage of the climate of wars and conflicts that is currently endemic in the Arab world to enrich itself, in an attempt to find a way out of its economic and social crisis. As for the Orientalists, they were experts in their field but they didn't understand Islam.

H: I think that what interested the Orientalists, whether we're talking about Corbin or Massignon, was mysticism or spirituality.

A: With one small nuance: they thought mysticism was part of Islam. That was their error. But mystical love has nothing to do with the Revelation. Look at the state of modern-day Islam. Without poetry, without mysticism and without philosophers, what is left? That which gives Islam its present cachet and presence is precisely that which Islam itself repudiated and refused.

H: In any case, the West prefers to deal with the question in a very superficial way. It may be that one day it will pay for its ignorance of Islam.

A: It has to rethink its relationship with others and with the Other.

Art, Myth, Religion

H: To describe the body in Arabic we have the words *al-jism* and *al-badan*. The latter is the erogenous, libidinal body. And you once told me that there is one thing that tempts you when you are tired, and that is watching a body dancing. You have a great love of dancing.

A: Dance is an art which, like poetry, gives the human being the possibility of separating himself from matter, in order better to see it, change it and understand it.

H: You very much liked *Carmen* by Carlos Saura, especially the face-to-face scene with the two women, Carmen and her rival.

A: Dance is purely human. Pure and naked. It is great art. And the face-to-face between the two dancers I see as a desire to present what is the most pure and the most naked. They each try to outdo each other when they say: 'I am the purest, it is I who embody that part of the human that has nothing to do with the human.' Each one says: 'I am more human than you and more "art" than you.' And watching a body dancing is to be faced with that which is purely you outside the materiality of the world.

H: In general, art for you, even when you are touching on elements of nature, is the art of transformation.

A: I was thrown into a world that I didn't know. By sheer chance I discovered something called 'art', 'poetry', which led me to the following question: 'Who am I?' Art in some way helps me to better know the place where I move, live and see my fellow humans. It helps me to better understand this universe I was thrown into.

H: 'Who am I?' This is a fundamental question for you. The question of the being who is not remote controlled but is free to explore, to know and to throw.

A: When I explore, my whole being is in it. As a consequence, I feel. There is joy and there is sorrow. There are a huge number of affects in the experience of exploring. The act of exploring brings about a change within the individual. An internal and perpetual change because it is a perpetual exploration. So writing is feeling and it is changing.

H: I hear the reader of Heraclitus and of Ibn ʿArabī who advocates perpetual change.

A: What survives in this ephemeral world is art and creativity. By definition, man is a creative creature who changes and transforms. I find myself propelled into human activity that is creation. What remains is the work of creation. Art bears witness that man is a great creator and that nature is the mother of all innovations. This explains the refusal of sculpture in Islam and the refusal of the image generally, even its destruction.

H: You have worked with some great painters and sculptors.

A: My interest in art dates from the 1950s. I was still living in Syria and I visited painters' studios. One day I made the acquaintance of Fātih al-Mudarris, who was a great painter in Damascus. Since then I have continued to forge links with painters, and have nourished and enriched myself from their work and personal contact with them. I have many artist friends with whom I have produced art books and catalogues, and even put on exhibitions. Shortly, I will be publishing a large volume on my relationships with Arab painters, which I have entitled *jamāliyat at-taḥawwul* (*The Aesthetics of Transformation*).

H: In the art of transformation there is in your work the conjugation of hand and spirit.

A: Indeed.

H: This conjugation of the hand and spirit has produced some collages. In your collages we find deconstruction. Nothing to do with Arab calligraphy. Beautiful, yes, but in black and white. This deconstruction reminds me of your text on Sabhan Adam where you explained how this artist broke with the 'He created man in His own image'. Sabhan

Adam produces a work of disfiguration. And this disfiguration touches you because it is art against religion.

A: In Sabhan Adam the being is a hybrid. The face and the body are deformed. It is a way to liberate the body from the aesthetic and religious codes that oppress it, a way to interrogate the humanity of the human and his animality too. The artist raises questions ducked by religion.

H: What is a form? What is an image? What is the truth of man? . . . These questions inspire you. You have always criticized 'the truth' preached by the Text. Your poetry is riddled with these questions.

A: Islam considers poetry a distraction and a deception with no connection to the truth.

H: Freud always praised 'the fine sensibility' of poets which allows them to see the hidden movements of the soul, and their courage in allowing the truth of the unconscious to speak. But it is this subjectivity that has difficulty in freeing itself from the weight of religion.

A: Islam killed poetry. This assassination, in fact, is that of subjectivity, of the individual's experience of life in favour of communal belief, that of the Ummah (the community). Islam rejects poetry as knowledge of, or search for, truth. It has banished it and condemned it. But poetry has no meaning if it ceases to be a search for truth. I may say that poetry is an unpicking and dismantling of religion, in its belief as much as in its knowledge. Because it is poetry that speaks the truth.

H: The Qur'an condemns the poets. Six verses attack poetry. One of them reads: 'And as to the poets, those who go astray follow them. / Do you not see that they wander about bewildered in every valley?'[1]

A: From a poetic point of view, religion is doubly nihilistic: it is a destruction of the beauty of existence on earth in order to replace it with the infinite padding of legends concerning paradise. Poetry has the advantage of directly confronting divinity without transforming itself into another religion. It is not ideological. Like mythology it questions and opens infinite horizons of research.

H: One day, by chance, you discovered a book on Adonis. It was the beginning of your interest in mythology.

A: It was an encounter with the force of creativity, the force that is universal in human beings.

H: Since then, Orpheus has become important to you, Narcissus questions you. And Ulysses? You seem to live out of a suitcase . . .

A: No sooner am I home that I am dreaming of the next journey.

H: You aren't Ulysses.

A: No, I'm not Ulysses. Ulysses is classical, traditional and a little romantic. In fact, he is quite ordinary. Of course, he has experienced adventures that others haven't experienced.

But he was no different from anyone else: when he was travelling he dreamed of coming home.

H: However, he did refuse the immortality that Calypso offered him in favour of another immortality.

A: He chose his home and his wife. For me, Ulysses doesn't pose any deep questions. He doesn't achieve mythical status. Myth is more complex, richer. Oedipus poses an infinity of questions, as do Orpheus and Narcissus. Ulysses was tested, he triumphed and he returned home. Ulysses represents a eulogy for the home.

H: He is the glorious self, or the heroic side of the self. He is not Orpheus.

A: What interests me in art and myth is the incessant questioning. Like myth, art asks questions. On the other hand, religion is an answer, as I have already said.

H: I understand your revolt against Islam. It opposes myth at the same time as poetry. But poetry talks of the existence of gods in the mythic mode. No language without myth.

A: The world existed before monotheism. It was plural and richer. To erase myth or art is to extinguish the flame of the human.

H: Art speaks the truth of the unconscious, it expresses the subjectivity of everyone. It is this truth, that of the unconscious, that has been insufficiently studied in our culture.

A: The years that followed the foundation of the Islam regime sounded the death knell for poetry, which didn't start to be reborn until the era of the Abbasids. In the same way the Text condemned creativity and the spirit of research, limiting the horizons of language and its freedom to speak of the world.

Poetry Between Language
and Precept

H: Although they wanted to create a modern poetry, the poets of the early twentieth century, such as Rusāfi, did not achieve it. Why is that, in your opinion?

A: We first of all need to agree what we mean by modernity. Modernity in France is different from modernity in the United States. But since we are talking about Arab modernity, what do we understand by that? Is it a poetic concept, or to do with thought or even everyday life?

H: We are talking about poetry.

A: To be modern in the Arab context is first of all to create a break with what has been said. A modern never remains in an inherited or dominant context. In poetry, modernity began with Bashshār ibn Burd and Abū Nuwās in the eighth century AD. They made a break with the poetic conception of the past. First of all, they broke with the religious world and the religious vision of the world, of things and of life. The means of expression became different.

H: Can we say that they created a new language?

A: Abū Nuwās and Bashshār ibn Burd invented the language of 'modern' life in Baghdad. This modernity reached a peak with al-Ma'arrī, who broke radically with the culture of certainty. But the poets of the early twentieth century, such as Rusāfi, wanted to introduce a modernity while preserving the classical and traditional modes of expression.

H: I understand better: he talked about locomotives, not camels, but in a style of yesteryear.

A: Rusāfi opted for a novelty, that is, the locomotive, but disregarded the spirit that invented it. Fundamentally he changed nothing. The poetry of the *nahḍa* (renaissance) is an imitation and repetition of the past. By choosing a locomotive, the poet has taken nothing from the West except material things, while forgetting what the great poets of the eighth, ninth and tenth centuries had realized, well before European modernity.

H: Our moderns are behind us. And Sayyāb?[1]

A: Sayyāb was the real start of modernity. He is the most important modern poet. Everything that came before him was a repetition and a pale imitation of the ancients. We can add Nizār Qabbānni, who created a new and free language, and Abdel Ṣabour, who broke with this classical eloquence by applying poetry to everyday life.[2] We could equally cite two great talents who passed away recently: Ounsi el-Hajj and Mohamed al-Maghout.[3] But the problem that has persisted to the present day is a lack of daring and a lack of initiative. The poets are afraid to make a proper break with the religious culture.

H: I'm beginning to understand what you mean by 'break with the religious culture'. I recall a poem by al-Ḥutay'a[4] about his mother, one in which he commits a veritable matricide. But the religious culture says: 'Paradise is below the feet of mothers'; it regards mothers as sacred. Al-Ḥutay'a, in another poem, speaks of a Narcissus who hates his face; what you rightly call subjectivity or human experience.

A: Al-Ḥutay'a belongs to the pre-Islamic era. We must talk about these poets just as modernity has talked about a Villon.[5] He is an avant-garde modern. Like Tarafa,[6] who was a great modern, or 'Imru'u l-Qays offering the image of a woman taking her pleasure with a man while breastfeeding her child. If Freud had read this poem he would have perhaps added things to his theory . . .

H: Psychoanalysis, described as a 'Copernican revolution', is fairly traditional when it comes to women. The image of 'Imru'u l-Qays represents a double pleasure: of the woman and of the mother. We had to wait until Mohamed Choukri's *Naked Bread* to dare to talk about the mother as a woman.

A: It's an extraordinary image. Pre-Islamic poetry was, like that of Bashshār ibn Burd and Abū Nuwās, a very modern space. Islam attacked this modernity and this creativity which draws deep on human experience. I deplore the fact that, to the present day, we in the Arab world don't have any deep studies of poetry, poetic language and Arab aesthetics.

H: I recall that you were the first to write a long article on Arab aesthetics, a piece on the words and concepts used to describe luxury. I translated it into French and it was published by the Colbert Committee.

A: I realized that there was nothing written on Arab aesthetics. I responded to the invitation to reflect upon the spiritual dimension of luxury in Arab society, on the Odyssey of words and their musicality.

H: The Odyssey of words in their love of things. I have read studies that have been written about your work or that of Mahmoud Darwish. The focus of interest is no longer the word but the thing that makes the poet speak.

A: Creating a thought involves a rending of the dominant culture. There are poets who have made breaks and opened a new space for poetical writing. Unfortunately, there aren't many of them. And Abū Nuwās, as I said, was more modern in the eighth century than many poets in the twentieth. He created another language and another world.

H: The Arab language is a gushing stream, according to you.

A: Because it is natural, and thereby universal. Universal and human. It is mythical as well because it was born naturally. It wasn't engendered by God. It wasn't created by Him or any being outside of the world. So, it is like a gushing spring . . .

H: From the earth?

A: From man, from the human, from the earth and the things of the cosmos. It is universal as well. It is religion that has limited it and de-universalized it. The poem gushed as if from a spring. It was like the wind, like the light or like the movement of the desert, like a plant or a palm. Pre-Islamic poetry was written outside of all dogma and all theorization. It was natural as it was the daughter of pure spontaneity. The theorizing of this led to meta-language.

H: Lacan talks about 'lalangue'[7] as a single word. The human is carried by language. When I hear the phrase 'maternal language' it strikes me that we don't have this expression in Arabic. Am I wrong?

A: The language of the 'culture' is the language of the father.

H: Could we say, then, that language is paternal and maternal?

A: That's right. The language of the culture is paternal and language of nature is the maternal language.

H: In other words, sonority, musicality, the first envelope . . .

A: Everything that is beyond reasoning, rationality and rationalization.

H: Why did you, who became Adonis, in your poem about your mother name her Um 'Alī? Before your mother, you become 'Alī again, rather than Adonis. It's like an appeal to that primary sonority and that envelope at the start of life.

A: I call her Um 'Alī in order to recognize something intimate, very personal, something connected to a cultural space and time. And I think it is more feminine to talk about Um 'Alī than Um Adonis. I call her Um 'Alī also to evoke the space in which she lived. In truth, Um 'Alī does not belong to Adonis. She belongs to 'Alī. Adonis is foreign, the other in me.

H: This poem is very powerful and very beautiful. You represent her speech, her look, her motherly and grandmotherly concerns with much love and, at the same time, a great deal of distance. In the poem we pick up the love of a son and the distance of an observer. It is a double movement.

A: In truth, I didn't think about that and didn't plan it. I am happy if this movement is perceptible.

H: You have always described your mother as the silent basis which is necessary for the poetic word to arrive. This is how I have always seen Um 'Alī or Um Adonis. When I read your poem I told myself that speaking about Um 'Alī is a way of restoring that first child, before the child became Adonis. Adonis is the cultural, plural child. 'Alī is the first child, her first child.

A: I like this as an explanation. You explain better than I why I kept the name Um 'Alī. I remain linked to my mother by the first name 'Alī, not by Adonis. Possibly it was also for me a way of seeing myself and seeing myself better through my mother's eyes.

H: The British psychoanalyst Winnicott defined the mother's face as a mirror for the child.

A: From the point of view of nature, we don't have two mothers. But you can have more than one father. The mother is the one who carries the baby. That is why the language closest to the creative human being is the language which is linked to maternity. That is why it is known as the 'mother tongue'.

H: You're talking here about the mother tongue (*lughat al-umm*). I think that there is a difference between the maternal language and the mother tongue in the sense that the maternal language is the language spoken by the mother. It is the words of the mother, her voice, the musicality of what she says . . . while in the expression 'mother tongue', language itself is the mother.

A: Absolutely. I am created by language as I am created by the mother.

H: In so-called medieval Arab society, Ibn 'Arabī, returning to myth, wrote: in the same way that Eve was created without a mother, Jesus was born without a father.

A: I agree in so far as we are in the universe of mythology. As a myth, it is fine.

H: If it wasn't a myth, he wouldn't have gone on to say: Adam and Mary are the parents, Jesus and Eve are brother and sister.

A: Because a religious Eve falsifies everything. Eve has to be like Adonis, like Ishtar: she is part of mythology.

H: This mother tongue never leaves you. Once you said that you have never written in French because the Arabic language demands great loyalty from you.

A: Absolute loyalty.

H: Would it be right to say that it is because of this loyalty that you do not experience the melancholy of exile? You have previously lived in the United States, taught in Geneva and have lived in France for a long time. Yet in spite of all these changes of place you don't strike me as an exile.

A: As long as I live in my language, as long as I have the feeling of this extraordinary mother tongue, I do not feel like an exile. Exile comes from politics, nationalism and ideology. Whereas, in the countries you mentioned, I have never had a feeling of exile. On the contrary, I have felt exile in my own country. Today, when I go back, I see Syria as a space like other spaces. There are specific elements, of course: the sun, the sea, family, friends ... But in an absolute sense, Syria, as a political and cultural regime, is just like any other country to me. Thus my essential problem is as follows: how might I know myself better through my language? My language is my country, my geography, my space, and it is the place in which I root myself.

H: Any roots, then, are roots in language. I think you have superbly and poetically defined 'lalangue'.

A: I am a creature of language. And I believe that language is not just about the word. It's another aspect of mythology. If I might take a leaf out of Lacan's book I might coin the phrase 'motology'[8] as a variation on mythology.

H: Mahmoud Darwish also said: 'I am my language.' He had lost everything: the earth, the tree, the well, the village . . . He had only the language in which he spoke of this loss, this tearing apart.

A: In a sense, yes, but he didn't separate his language from his land. Language and land are closely bound together for him. Because the land was bound together with a cause.

H: Not a national cause. It was the freedom of a whole people.

A: Indeed.

H: Would I be right in saying that the fact that you didn't have this national cause allowed you to move to a more universal dimension?

A: When I was younger I was interested in ideologies and I was politically active. Nowadays, and perhaps because I was born before Mahmoud Darwish, I have moved beyond ideologies. Man is my problem and the universe itself is my cause. There is a type of freedom connected to a cause, a politics or a people, let's call it a social or historical freedom, and a freedom which has nothing to do with the freedom to travel, to love . . . I would say: as long as the human being is not free on this earth, humanity is not free. A Frenchman can't be free, in a deep sense, if a Palestinian is a prisoner or deprived of liberty. Freedom is human, and the human being is responsible for the freedom of every human being.

H: You give exile a very subtle meaning. This leads me to the question on Islam and the dimension of exile. In *Moses and Monotheism*, Freud advances the idea that the foundation cannot do without the figure of the foreigner. To simplify, Arab writers say that Islam began with an exile.

A: In Islam, there is no real exile. The displacement from Mecca to Medina wasn't an exile. It was the same country, the same language, the same traditions. There is no hint of wandering. The displacement here has none of the nobility implied by the word 'exile'. A tribe which goes from one place to another, or which escapes enemies and finds itself with another tribe that is welcoming and generous, does not cross this dimension of exile.

H: So it is to do with the same structure. And Tabarī says that the first Muslims, not knowing how to date events, chose to start their calendar from the arrival of the Meccans in Medina. Thus, for a practical question, from memory.

A: Of course. Moreover, when they changed location, the Quraysh acquired a greater strength. You might even say that they moved in order to defeat both emigration and exile. The displacement was in the name of victory and domination. Exile involves a rending, a journey, trials and tribulations. But when the first Muslims changed location they reinforced their power and domination.

H: You often quote the verse of Abū Tammām: 'In your exile, your renaissance' or 'Exile yourself in order to renew yourself.'

A: It is beyond a political cause. It is experience centred on the human.

H: In the verse we find the word *ghurba*, the fact of being a foreigner, with all that that entails in terms of enfeeblement, foreignness, nostalgia, distress . . .

A: Quite. But in the context we are discussing, the journey from Mecca to Medina, it is more like an invasion, a transfer to acquire more power.

H: Might we even say: with the arrival of the Quraysh at the home of the Anṣār in Medina, and bearing in mind how successful the incomers were, the real exiles were the Anṣār?

A: Absolutely. The Anṣār were denied, denigrated as if they had done nothing for Islam and for the Prophet of Islam. They welcomed the Quraysh, opened their hearts and their homes, they fed them. They gave them shelter and defended Muhammad against the Meccans. And in return: total rejection. The Quraysh took over as if the Anṣār had never existed. 'Umar said: *an-nubuwwa fī banī Hāshim* (prophecy is in the hands of Banū Hāshim[9]) and the caliphate is for the other people of Quraysh. It was a division in a single tribe. One side of the Quraysh has prophecy and the other side, power. In fact, it is the triumph of sameness. The Anṣār were the losers.

H: So they experienced a genuine interior exile.

A: At the very least, they were rejected.

H: I understand that the Quraysh didn't have this experience of exile because they had taken with them into the welcoming country the language of love and power. Exile can be a form of intermingling, an opening-up to the other, but it can also be devastating.

A: Exile is a consciousness and a culture. A man without culture cannot feel or understand what exile is.

H: Nevertheless, this man can be undermined by being torn away from his land and his language.

A: To be far away from family, friends, your old house . . . this is the everyday level of the feeling of exile. In my sense, we can't talk about exile in the absolute. Exile is an experience of life, of culture, of language, of relationship with others. You can't generalize. To each his own exile. There are people who seek exile and who want to distance themselves from the milieu into which they were born; others hate the language and look for another language; and there are individuals who don't have a choice. In this case it is an imposed or forced exile.

H: In *Mawsim al-hijra ilā ash-shamāl* (*Season of Migration to the North*),[10] a Sudanese exile loses himself in the image that the European has of Arabs. On his return, he vividly experiences what Khatibi puts in words: 'Returning to one's country is a beautiful illusion. You never return home, you return to the circle of its shadow.'[11]

A: There is no exile in the absolute. We have to be clear: as in this case. Personally I don't feel like an exile as long as I have friendship, love, as long as the other exists. As long as there is creativity, I don't feel that I am in exile.

H: I have never detected any melancholy of exile in you, as it happens; but a very strong sensory attachment to the land: when you take oil, for example, to sprinkle on certain dishes, when you have your coffee, when you have your cheese, that is, when you rediscover those primary sensory objects.

A: It's what I feel with respect to things I have known. It is the habit of the body too. To be more precise, I would say: I always want to see again the place where I walked for the first time.

Beyond *Al-Kitāb*

H: *Al-Kitāb* testifies to the engagement of the writer and poet that you are. History is usually written by the victors. You write another history, that of the rebels. You restore humanity to the people who were exterminated, you recall the names of the disappeared and you give them a voice. And, to adopt the phrase of Janine Altounian, you have given them a 'shroud' so that they no longer need to be wandering, tormented souls.

A: True history is that of the vanquished. It is the banished, the condemned and the marginalized who created our literature, our poetry, our imaginary and our philosophy. They are the ones who created the aura of this culture.

H: *Al-Kitāb* is the initiation of a new genre. But it is above all a new discourse in the sense that history might be written and read differently. It is a first.

A: It is a first in the history of the Arabs.

H: As an analyst, I was very interested in your way of relating events in the form of repetitions. You repeat the names of individuals, places, the word *rāwiya* (the narrator, teller) as attempts to give psychic form to what has been imprisoned or encysted in the blank of memory. You repeat until the psyche, little by little, manages to think the event. It is a way of inscribing a meaning.

A: It is what I have done in all my writings, whether poetry or essays. I wanted to lift the veil on this history that isn't talked about and to say that there is a camouflaged, hidden history, which should be known about. There are many events that need to emerge from the shadows, many facts that should be related. I made a choice. Having said that, the essential idea is this: you can't write a new history without calling into question our way of approaching the past. We have to review our past and look at it from a new conception of the world. The Arab world has refused to do this. But without this new view, our culture risks disappearing altogether.

H: *Al-Kitāb* is subversive. Not only because you are opposed to religious discourses but because you dismantle the discourses which have governed us up to the present day. Subversive because it also dismantles a way of speaking. The poet, who criticizes the religious idea of hell, does not hesitate to descend into the abysses of history and of being. I read the works that you bring me back from Lebanon. And I ask myself: how come a disaster like that happening now hasn't produced a great literature? Perhaps we're in a state of shock and it is too soon to think about the disaster; perhaps the Arab 'being' is so torn, in conflict with the father, the mother and all the figures sacralized by religious discourse, that it doesn't have the psychic luxury to produce a literature.

A: These are two very good ideas. Together, they might explain the situation of Arab culture. This is the reason why I say and say again: the reigning Arab culture arises from psychology. It is fertile territory for psychoanalysts.

H: My elders dreamed of a Marx, but we have even more need of a Freud. And I understand why Freud has not yet been admitted into the intellectual fabric of the Arab world.

A: Psychoanalysis is essentially anti-religious. It is exploration, eulogy and subjectivity.

H: You told me that you had started to write a follow-up to *Al-Kitāb*.

A: Yes. It's my testament. My testament in poetic form.

H: Why a follow-up to *Al-Kitāb*?

A: I don't know how to speak about my work. And I don't like doing it. But I will say that, since *Ath-thābit wa'l mutaḥawwil*, I have been trying to instigate a new reading of our corpus, to encourage searchers and readers towards a new critical vision. I discovered that our whole history was falsified, completely fabricated, and that those who created the Arab civilization and its grandeur were banished, condemned, rejected, imprisoned, even crucified. We have to reread this civilization and see it differently: with a new gaze and with a new humanity.

H: If I might borrow the expression of Michel de Certeau, you invite us to transform history-legend into history-work. It takes courage to tear oneself free of what Freud called the 'fairy tales of religion'.

A: Freud was a great man, an innovator who had an enormous amount of courage. You need courage and honesty to reread a history full of lies, fabrications and falsifications.

H: Adonis! You are the author of a monumental work, you are admired and known and recognized around the world. You love Orpheus. Orpheus lost Eurydice. What have you lost?

A: The question that haunts me is the following: when Orpheus descended into the underworld, was it purely to see Eurydice?

H: It is true that we do not stop to consider the different facets of myth and reflect upon them. And as you say, myth is a question that is eternally open. But you, what have you lost? My professional conditioning leads me to think of the primary loss. But to say that it is the loss of the mother as oedipal love object makes both psychoanalysis and loss banal.

A: We have to distinguish the living mother, the mother as presence, from the mother as symbol, idea or imaginary. I can say that I have lost the presence of the mother, the body of the mother. On the other hand, I have gained, by transforming this presence into symbol and into imaginary. She is now more present than ever. And so I am more rich in her. Full of her, more than ever.

H: This transformation has been with you always. The tears of your mother became the bridge of tears in your poem. As I said, I have never detected any melancholy in you. On the contrary, you manage to transform the small piece of wood, the pebble or your mother's tears into a poetic creation.

A: As far as I'm concerned, I can't speak of a loss that has created a state of melancholy, but rather of a movement of questioning and permanent searching: 'Who am I?' I think that is the most important question of my life. It is the question of my presence in life. How has my life been built this way? What role has chance played in my life? In fact, my whole life has been nothing more than a chain of surprises and chance events. My life has been orchestrated by something extraordinary. But today I feel that I have lost my old age. I haven't succeeded in transforming it into another childhood.

H: In truth, I have tried to understand this movement of creativity of yours since the beginning of your work. What are its fundamentals?

A: I can say that I have lost my father, that I have lost many friends. But in reality I feel that all I have lost is my old age. I will not be able to realize that which I dreamed about.

H: Might this be a loss in advance?

A: It is a dreamed or imagined loss.

H: You talk about your work as incomplete?

A: I do talk about incompletion. There is nothing to lose in this world. We shouldn't give loss a sociological or political meaning. Yes, I have lost my native town, my house, friends who have died . . . But this is not real loss. Because, poetically speaking, there is not something in this world that deserves the name of loss. We are thrown into the world and lost in it from the very start. The biggest loss is of myself, in advance, since I was thrown into this world without being asked. I never had the choice.

H: I am constantly the victim of my professional conditioning and I think about the loss of the breast, for example. Nevertheless, listening to you, I told myself that we mustn't objectify loss.

A: The loss of the breast is not a real loss. On the contrary, it is a gain. I have the poetic freedom to not accept this explanation.

H: And you are right. The poet is always further ahead than the analyst. The non-separation from the breast is a psychic catastrophe. But, for your poetic freedom, can I say: might loss be the fact that the word can never say what the human really feels?

A: That's it, you're getting there. Perhaps this impotence of language or the impotence of the human to define things.

And my rejection of religions and ideologies stems from the fact that they all claim to speak the absolute truth. But it's to do with a great lack. It's about a lack and not a loss. There is always a lack.

H: If there is something great it is in the thing. The word is, by definition, impotent. Is that it?

A: That's a good summary. Religious thought says the opposite: the word says the thing once and for all. And that is why I say that Islam has limited language. Language before Islam was beautiful and free. Islam restricted its possibilities, its extent and its horizons. But the word can never say a thing once and for all. I call that a wound.

H: Is this 'the wound of the proper name' as Abdelkébir Khatibi puts it?

A: It is rather the wound of the world.

H: I now better understand your critiques vis-à-vis the monotheist texts and the simplistic readings of those texts. In fact, as well as the precepts, you challenge the triumph of the word.

A: Religion cheats and preaches the omnipotence of the word. That is a betrayal of the human being.

H: In fact, what you have been denouncing since *Ath-thābit wa'l mutaḥawwil* is the sovereignty of the word.

A: I repeat: poetry, like myth, is a question. Religion is an answer.

H: . . . which is the misfortune of the question.

How to Conclude?

H: I am thinking about the title of the novel by the South African writer Alan Paton, *Cry, the Beloved Country*. This was in 1948. Since then, apartheid has been abolished. I want to hold on to the hope.

A: What has happened in the Arab countries since 2011 is a sort of return to before-man, to savagery. A man can be killed for stealing or because he thinks differently. They kill those who aren't Sunni or who think differently. This displays a hatred for the human. These practices and the silence of Muslims around them show that Muslims, as I have already said, believe and think that Islam is the only true religion, the complete religion, the one that God has chosen for His faithful – as if it were impossible to live without Islam. How can you think that a world without Islam would be a world without meaning?

H: The events that we see today raise questions about those of yesterday. But I would rather hold on to hope for the generations to come. This book is a contribution to that.

A: You are right to hope. But let us ask ourselves this: can the Arabs release or liberate themselves from dominant Islam? And would the Arab language be able to liberate itself from the Revelation? Is it possible to have another reading of Islam, a reading advocating equality between men without distinction? Is it possible to have a reading that speaks of religion without seeing itself as the Truth? The truth that is imposed by force is a destruction of human consciousness and life. And a society that doesn't dare express itself freely is not a human society. Humans are human because they have a right to freedom and knowledge. If you take away this right, you take away their humanity.

H: Some authors are starting nevertheless to question the fundamentals of our culture.

A: History as related by the chroniclers is a collection of legends and stories in contradiction with thought, reflection and science. Indeed, some authors are already applying themselves to this task. The task is to rethink and reconsider the themes and questions not dealt with in the Arab world and re-address them in a radical and a liberating way. You have noticed the absence of works such as those of the emir 'Abd el-Qāder in his own country. We need to ask questions: why this failure of mystical thought and the failure of spirituality in Arab culture today? This is an important and inescapable question for anyone who truly wants to know this culture.

H: We have to reflect on the drives underlying the foundation of Islam. Daesh reminds us of the repressed that we have neglected and which has transformed itself into an encysted thing.

A: My hope is that Daesh is the death rattle of this Islam. Like a candle that sputters just before it goes out. And this is what is happening right now in the Arab world. The Arabs are devouring each other. They slit throats, exterminate, humiliate . . . Daesh exterminates Shi'ites, Yazidis, Sunnis . . . It is a history of the dirt. I no longer wish to talk about what is called Arab history. I don't talk about Arabs any more except in the field of poetry. Arabs haven't succeeded in creating a state or instituting citizenship. Thanks to incomprehensible circumstances, which we have tried to elucidate, the Arabs have succeeded in fabricating this Arab history. But I believe that the context in which the Arab has lived for fifteen centuries is at an end. We have to understand that peoples die and civilizations die too. This Ummah no longer has a creative presence in any field of human civilization. The Arabs are absent from the world. It is death.

H: Could we, in spite of everything, retain a glimmer of hope and repeat the words of Nietzsche: 'One must still have chaos in oneself to be able to give birth to a dancing star'?[1] This disaster will, perhaps, incite us to reflect on our history.

A: The chaos is there. It is possible that the younger generations are creating another space by breaking radically with the Arab context. Perhaps they will succeed in creating another history and another world. We can talk of hope in this sense. But there could be no hope in a continuity based on the Arab past. As there have been individuals who have distinguished themselves by their creativity during these centuries, there will always be people to create another world or even another Islam. Why not? But not in continuity. We need a radical break.

H: In any case, the Arab faces the obligation to reflect and draw lessons. He scarcely has any choice.

A: The Muslim individual has to grasp that he or she can't continue to be a cog in the gigantic machine that is the community. Luckily there is a movement in the Arab world which is starting to reclaim atheism or the freedom not to practise religion.

H: In Morocco, young people have demonstrated to express their desire not to observe Ramadan, the non-observance of which can lead to imprisonment. We have to live through Daesh to finally reflect on the past and its foundations.

A: The disaster of today can accelerate the birth of a new consciousness. But we're paying a high price for it.

H: Hearing you say 'accelerate', I think about Boris Vian: 'As long as they leave me time enough.'² It is too sad. When my family enrolled me in school, there was this hope of a better future. But we have marched into the future with the vision of the ancients, like Rusāfi talking about locomotives in the way the Ancients talked about camels. I sometimes get the feeling that studying, instead of liberating us, has reinforced the split self.

A: That's why our culture needs real work. This regression is unprecedented in human history. The situation of the Arab world is catastrophic if we think about the people and not the wealth with which it overflows. Of course, peoples are extinguished, but in a noble manner. But we are dying in an ignoble manner. Islam is reduced to a sort of granary where the Muslim replenishes himself. We have to rethink all this.

H: There is the violence of the texts which are sacralized and the violence of the West as a political institution which has played an important role in the break-up of the Arab left.

A: It's further proof that present-day Arabs are the absolute allies of those who have oppressed them for centuries: France, Britain and Turkey. They have ended up in bed with the very same forces that have immolated them. And today, these wars between Shi'ites and Sunnis express the scale of the catastrophe. One side is the enemy of the other. It is crazy. Yemen is being assaulted in the most atrocious manner.

H: We have to rethink fratricide and historical memory. Yemen is the country of Bilqīs. And, economically, Mecca depended on this part of the Arab peninsula.

A: Past-memory is a gaping wound, a catastrophe at the core of Arab life. Culturally, obscure; humanly, savage; morally, debasing. It is a wound to the heart and the spirit.

H: Abdul Rahman Munif, in *Riḥlatu ḍaw'* (*Journey of a Light*),[3] insists on a writing that is not borrowed, a personal writing of our questions, and says also that history is not a collection of past events, but a present that attests to our choices and our capacity to transform it for a better future.

A: Present-day Arab society is a collection of institutions of violence and torture, institutions of 'decay', to use the expression of Michel de Certeau. And the Muslim Arab man today does not live like a free and cultured man but like a machine or a number within a mass which calls itself the 'group', 'community', 'confession' or 'tribe'. The Arab intellectual has the task not of saving memory, but of saving us from the past and from memory.

H: Memory preserves like blocks that which has never been thought because it was sacralized by the precepts and a language that vaunts, in the split, torture and the precepts. The psychological dimension has always been obscured. But it turns out to be decisive in order to finally have done with sacralization. This sacralization itself constitutes a violence, because it takes away the possibility of de-idealizing a transmitted corpus that hasn't been thought.

A: Psychoanalysis will eventually, I hope, deconstruct the legend on which Islam rests. But let us leave that for another conversation.

A Last Word

Against essentialism: the notion of progress in the Islamic conception of man and the world

The conception of man and the world that predominates in Islam rests on three pillars.

Firstly: Islamic prophecy is the last of the prophecies. And the Prophet of Islam is the ultimate prophet. He himself put it: 'No prophet after me.'

Secondly: the truths transmitted by this prophecy concerning the celestial world and the terrestrial, human world are ultimate truths. There is no other truth that might deny them. On the other hand, anything that does not contradict these truths or is not contradicted by them is acceptable.

Thirdly: man cannot modify or change what the Revelation has said. His sole duty is to believe and obey, to practise it. If we push the logic further, we can say that God himself has nothing more to reveal. He has said his last word to his last prophet: 'Religion is Islam.' So we understand the statement: 'Islam eradicates what went before, except those things in agreement with it.' Everything that doesn't agree with it, it rejects. Islam eradicates not only that which went before, but that which comes after.

Religion is the criterion of justice for what came before and what will come after.

The Muslim man, he who lives in the religion of Islam, is the man par excellence, according to God. Following this logic, we can see that Revelation governs reason. Muslim reason eradicates all anterior forms of reason. Muslim judgement and criteria, once they benefit from the Revelation, also eradicate preceding and future criteria and judgements.

Thus we see that, in this conception, man derives his human essence only from the Islamic revelation. Islam defines this human essence, which comes from God and not from man himself; from the Revelation and not from culture, experiences, life; from the word of God, and therefore not from the words of humans.

If we take up the idea of the relationship between essence and existence as formulated by Sartre, 'existence precedes essence', this states the exact opposite of the Islamic concept, according to which essence precedes existence, since human essence comes from God. Islam is real human nature. As such, it is clear that Islam is an essentialism. That might explain that the other, the non-Muslim, in the Islamic conception, has the choice between two identities: either s/he is an unbeliever, and so must be rejected or even killed; or s/he lives under the aegis of the Islamic regime and, in this case, s/he pays a tribute.

If man's essence precedes his existence, it follows that man does not create his personality; he has no impact on the order of the world. He tries to imitate, in his life and work, the prototype represented by the life of the Prophet and of his closest companions. The life of Muslims is not characterized by creation but by mimicry and repetition. There is no freedom for man, only an invitation to repeat. Each creation is a heresy. Each heresy leads to hell.

As the Imam Shāfi'ī said: 'Anyone who explains the Qur'an by expressing a personal opinion is wrong, even if he is right.' It is not the role of the individual to have an opinion on this subject: only the community must pass comment. But, as Sartre said, man is by necessity free, because his essence is freedom. According to the Islamic vision, however, man is necessarily an imitator and must respect tradition. He has no freedom. He is obliged to live, think and work by embodying his Muslim essence. Man cannot be man without Islam. To be a Muslim means abandoning all individuality and dissolving your identity in the community. There is no subjectivity in Islam.

Yet progress is above all a project. It is an essentially human work. Man himself is a project, according to the humanist tradition, of which Sartre is the great modern representative. A project presupposes leaving the past and heading from the present towards the future. Every project implies a vision of the future and contains a tendency towards something finer and more human. In Sartre's words, 'Man is a movement towards the future.' He creates his own essence, realizes his own project, without constraint, particularly of the religious kind.

In Islam the movement is necessarily turned towards the past. The future has no sense and exists only in the light of the past: the past is the future of the present. This is how we are meant to understand 'progress' according to Islam: the practice of imitation and this ideal of the past. The past is the place of truth - in other words, to engage in progress is to Islamicize the future, based on the past. The project of progress in the Islamic vision is to Islamicize the world.

Thus we understand why Islam is a religion indissolubly linked with power. This power is essentially religious, at the opposite pole to secular civil life. Islam is a movement with the aim of transforming the here and now into religion: culture, in its artistic, scientific and human forms, is instrumentalized to defend this power. Thus the Muslim believes that he still lives in the light of the origin. He separates himself from time to head towards the eternity of paradise.

The paradox is that the peoples who have lived under Islamic influence have achieved great things despite the religious constraints. They have made progress in life, poetry, art, thought, philosophy and science, even though in constant conflict with these constraints. Some of them paid with their lives or the destruction of their work, or with being marginalized.

What is striking in this paradox is that among the creators, especially those in philosophy and poetry, there isn't a single follower of traditional Islam, the Islam of power. There is no great poet, over the course of fourteen centuries, or a single great philosopher, who believed in the Islam of power or the Islam of the Law.

All were in agreement, in one way or another, with what the great poet al-Ma'arrī had to say: 'There are two sorts of people on earth. Those who have a religion but no reason; those who don't have a religion but have reason.'

That is why, from this perspective, the meaning and essence of man does not come from his humanity but from his religion – i.e. Islam. And if a Muslim abjures his religion, he loses his human essence. He will be condemned, killed. Man is created to be a Muslim and to serve Islam.

To be more precise: the predominant conception in Islam today still maintains that Islam is the sole source of truths. The problem would perhaps not reside in these truths themselves if they were individual and only involved the individual. The problem is that these totalizing and closed truths are imposed on culture, society and humanity. They represent absolute criteria for building a society, even if there are other components, other religions in this society.

Truth in Islam is a truth-community. It comes from the Creator, not from any creature. Thus it is unchanging. It is transmitted from generation to generation, total and definitive, like a spiritual inheritance. Its meaning establishes the secret of existence. If it is abandoned, existence itself is finished. It has no meaning without these truths. To defend them is to defend God and to defend existence, even against itself.

If we consider truth as an individual question, involving only the person who believes it, then we can accept it as an expression of freedom. When it is defined as social and total, involving the whole of society, then it is imposed by the Law. That is why it becomes a form of violence. Believing in it becomes an act of submission. At that moment, society has no truth. Truth possesses society. The Text is higher than reality. It becomes the master of reality, which is its slave. The truth becomes a perpetual war against thought and against man – against the truths of others.

From this perspective, progress would be a total imitation of origins. According to the Western tradition from Aristotle to Hegel, imitation has no meaning if it adds nothing new.

Imitation is a supplement to what is imitated. Otherwise, imitation would be nothing more than a superficial copy and a deformation. It is this imitation, this deformation, that the Arabs are living in our era.

Progress is human work, based on creation and invention. It is closely connected to the future. The culture that considers the future as nothing more than a rewriting of the past doesn't see real progress. Unfortunately, as long as such a vision holds sway in Arab society, the only thing that will advance is regression.

By definition, man is a creative creature. He always goes further, in life, in society and even in language. The future is the space where the energies and powers of man are realized in order to master the universe and better understand its secrets.

The predominant conception today requires a new reading of Islam and of the cultures of the peoples who have lived under the aegis of Islamic power; it also necessitates a new reading of Arab culture in its entirety, the writing of a new history; finally, it necessitates founding new relationships between words and things, man and the world, man and progress.

Glossary

'adhrā	virgin (feminine term)
'arḍ	honour
āla	machine
al-badan	the body in its erogenous dimension
al-ghussāq	boiling water in torture
al-ijmā'	consensus
al-jism	the body
lughat al-umm	mother-language
an-nār	fire
an-nisā	women
Anşār	the people of Medina who welcomed and supported Muhammad
'aşr an-nahḍa	renaissance
batsch	oppression, tyranny
burqa	full-length veil
faqīh	jurist
fatwa	edict
fiqh	jurisprudence

firaq bāṭinīya	Batinites, a movement that appeared in 205, 250 or 276 Hijri Era. It gave birth to a number of groups, including the Qarmatians. They were considered as heretics.
fitna	war between Muslims
fuqahā	theologians
futūḥāt	conquests
ghanā'im	spoils of war
ghassa	food of torture
ghurba	estrangement, exile
Ḥadīth	word of Muhammad
hāwiya	the abyss
ḥarth	field of labour
ḥurūb ar-rida	wars of Apostasy
ḥouri	woman of paradise
ijtihād	interpretation of legal experts
ilāh	divinity
istibāḥa	licentiousness
Jabbār	the Almighty
jahannam	Gehenna
Jāhilīya	pre-Islamic era
janna	paradise
jihad	holy war
kufr	non-belief
lazā	hell
Mu'allaqāt	pre-Islamic poetry
Mu'tazilites	movement of thinkers which formed from the first half of the second century Hijri Era in Basra and became a speculative school of the first order

Qarmatians	dissident political movement of the Fatimid dynasty, fourth century Hijri Era
Quraysh	the tribe of Muhammad
raḥma	mercy
rāwiya	narrator, teller of tales
saby	taking prisoners of war
saqqār	hellfire
Saqīfa	a place near Medina where, after the death of Muhammad, discussions took place concerning his succession
shar'	the Law
Sharia	body of Islamic law
sinnu l'ya's	menopause
tābi'	follower, disciple of the Muslim doctrine
Ummah	the community of the faithful
Wahhabism	Saudi politico-religious movement founded by Muhammad ben Abdelwahhab in the thirteenth century which preaches a puritan and rigorous form of Islam
wathan	idol
Zinj	the Blacks; the revolt of the Zinj took place in 225 Hijri Era under the reign of the Abbassids

Notes

A Spring Without Swallows

1 The Revolt of the Zinj began in 225 Hijri Era (during the reign of the Abbasids). The rebels were revolting against social and economic discrimination. They founded a state south of Basra but were defeated by the existing powers.

2 A dissident movement during the Fatimid dynasty which created a state in 899 AD. The Qarmatians founded a socialist doctrine based on respect for work and a fair distribution of money. They entered Mecca in 317 Hijri Era and seized the Black Stone; they restored it only twenty years later on payment of a large ransom. They were finally exterminated in 1027 AD.

3 Movements considered as extremely dangerous because heretical.

4 Abū Nuwās was of Persian origin. He lived in the palaces of Hārūn al-Rashīd and his two sons. He died in 192/813 (note double dating system: Hijri calendar / Christian calendar).

5 Abū aṭ-Ṭayyib Aḥmad ibn al-Ḥusayn al-Jūfī, known as

al-Mutanabbī, born in Kufa and assassinated while returning from Baghdad in 354/965.

6 Al-Ma'arrī: poet and philosopher, born in Syria in 363/973,
died in 449/1057.

The Necessity of Rereading: History and Identity

1 Marcel Detienne, *L'Identité nationale, une énigme* (Paris:
Gallimard 'Folio', 2010).

2 Tabarī: historian and theologian. Born in Tabaristan, probably in 839 AD, died in Baghdad in 923.

3 Ibn Kathīr: commentator on the Qur'an. Born in Syria in
701 Hijri Era, died in 774 Hijri Era.

4 Saqīfa: a place to the northwest of the mosque at Medina,
where the Muslims gathered after the death of Muhammad
to choose a new leader for the Muslim community.

5 Adonis, *Ath-thābit wa'l mutahawwil*, 4 volumes (Beirut:
Dār As-Sāqī, 1973).

6 Averroes (Ibn Rushd): born in Cordoba in 520/1126, died
in 1198 in Marrakesh. An important commentator on
Aristotle.

7 Alhazen (Ibn al-Haytham): one of the principal Arab
mathematicians and unquestionably the greatest physi-
cian. Born in Basra in 354/965, he died in 420/1039.

8 Ibn 'Arabī: mystic and author of a huge body of work. Born
in 560/1165 in Murcia, died in Damascus in 638/1240.

9 The Mu'tazilites: a group that formed in the first half of
the second century Hijri Era in the town of Basra and
constituted a school of speculative thought of the highest
order.

10 Avicenna (Ibn Sīnā): born in 370/980. His native language
was Persian. Died in Hamadan in 428/1037.

11 Ibn Rawandī: born in 210 Hijri Era, died at the age of forty.

He was initially a Mu'tazilite before becoming a dissident. One of the great atheist thinkers of Islam.

12　It was Moustapha Ziwar who introduced psychoanalysis into the Arab world, founding the first faculty of psychology (at the University of Ayn Shams in Cairo). Born in Egypt in 1907, he died in 1990.

13　Abū Bakr: companion of Muhammad and his father-in-law. He became the first caliph.

14　'Umar: father-in-law of Muhammad and the second caliph after Abū Bakr.

15　The *Mu'allaqāt*: pre-Islamic verses.

16　Moustapha Safouan, *Why Are the Arabs Not Free? The Politics of Writing* (Oxford: Wiley-Blackwell, 2007).

Rethinking the Fundamentals

1　*Futūḥ al-Buldān*, by Aḥmād ibn Yaḥyā ibn Djābīr ibn Dāw-Balādhurī. Died probably in 279 Hijri Era.

2　Edward Chiéra, *Les Tablettes babyloniennes* (Paris: Payot, 1940).

3　Qur'an 2:217. The first number indicates the Sura, the second indicates the verse. Quotations are taken from *The Holy Qur'an*, translated by M. H. Shakir and published by Tahrike Tarsile Qur'an, Inc., in 1983.

4　Qur'an 3:4.

5　Qur'an 4:56.

6　Fakhr al-Dīn al Rāzī was a historian and theologian. Born in Iran in 1149, he died in Afghanistan in 1209.

7　Qur'an 3:85.

8　Qur'an 5:3.

9　Qur'an 71:26.

10　Qur'an 7:136.

11　Qur'an 44:16.

12 Qur'an 17:97.

13 Qur'an 17:21.

14 Qur'an 33:66.

15 Qur'an 22: 19–22.

16 Word of Muhammad.

17 Tabarī, *Tārīkh* (*Chronicles*), vol. 9, p. 125.

18 Qur'an 14:50.

19 Tabarī, *Tārīkh* (*Chronicles*), vol. 4, p. 145.

20 Qur'an 40:71–2.

21 Qur'an 69:30–2.

22 Tabarī, *Tārīkh* (*Chronicles*), vol. 12, p. 220.

23 Cf. Preface to Adonis, *Al-Kitāb II* (Paris: Seuil, 2012).

24 Qur'an 73:12–13.

25 Tabarī, *Tārīkh* (*Chronicles*), vol. 12, p. 289.

26 Qur'an 44:43–6.

27 Qur'an 44:51–3.

28 Qur'an 37: 64–5.

29 Qur'an 47:15.

30 Ibid.

31 Qur'an 38:57.

32 Tabarī, *Tārīkh* (*Chronicles*), vol. 10, p. 598.

33 Qur'an 35:36.

34 Qur'an 4:168–9.

35 Qur'an 50:30.

36 Ibn Hishām, *As-sīra an-nabawīya* (*The Biography of the Prophet Muhammed*), vol. 2, p. 636.

37 Tabarī, *Tārīkh* (*Chronicles*), vol. 3, p. 423.

38 Al-Wāqidī, *The Book of Conquests*, p. 8.

39 Ibid., vol. 3, pp. 879–80.

40 Suyūṭī, *Nuzhat al-majālis*, pp. 122–3.

41 D. H. Lawrence, *Apocalypse* (Cambridge: Cambridge University Press, 2002).

42 The phrase was coined by Gilles Deleuze in an essay refer-
ring to D. H. Lawrence. Cf. Gilles Deleuze, 'Nietzsche
and Saint Paul, Lawrence and John of Patmos', in *Essays
Critical and Clinical*, trans. Daniel W. Smith and Michael
A. Greco (Minneapolis: University of Minnesota Press,
1997), p. 37. [*Trans.*]

43 Acts of the first conference of Arabic-language psychoanalysts which was held on 20–23 May 2004 at the Palais de
l'Unesco: *La Psyché dans la culture arabe et son rapport à la
psychanalyse* (Beirut: Dār al-Fārābī, 2004).

44 Centre International de Recherches et Etudes Trans-
disciplinaires (International Centre for Transdisciplinary
Research and Studies). [*Trans.*]

45 Guillaume de Lorris and Jean de Meung, *Le Roman de
la Rose*, thirteenth century. English translation from *The
Romance of the Rose*, trans. Frances Horgan (Oxford:
Oxford University Press, 1994), p. 3.

46 Rābi'a was the first female mystic in Islam. Born in Basra
and died in 135 Hijri Era.

47 The youngest of Muhammad's wives.

48 Qur'an 33:33.

49 Adonis, *Al-Kitāb* (Paris: Seuil, 2007), p. 28.

50 Al-Ḥallāj: the most famous mystic in the history of
Islam. Born in 244/858 in Fars, died by crucifixion in
309/922.

51 Qur'an 2:223.

52 Qur'an 4:34.

53 Qur'an 4:3.

54 Qur'an 4:11.

55 Qur'an 4:34.

56 Qur'an 2:228.

57 Fāṭima: woman celebrated by 'Imru'u l-Qays; Khawla is

the beloved in the poem by Tarafa; Maïa is likewise in the poem by Abū Tammān. See *Le Diwân de la poésie classique*, trans. Houria Abdelouahed and Adonis (Paris: Gallimard, 2008).

58 See *Le Dīwân de la poésie classique*.

59 A phrase of Ibn 'Arabī.

60 Daughter of Muhammad.

61 Al-'Arjī is a poet from the Umayyad period, died in 120/738. Imprisoned for leading a 'debauched' life, he remained locked up until his death.

62 May Ziade: Lebanese writer, essayist and journalist, pioneer of Eastern feminism. Born in 1886 in Nazareth, died in 1941.

63 Huda Sha'rawi: feminist writer. Born in Egypt in 1879, died in 1947 in Cairo.

64 Qāsim Amīn: of Kurdish origin, writer and essayist known as 'Muḥarrir al-mar'a', the 'liberator of women'. Born in Egypt in 1863, he died in 1908.

65 Samira 'daughter of the Arab peninsula' and 'Ā'isha 'daughter of the shore'.

66 Qur'an 56:35–6.

67 *Allāt Allāh āla.* اللات الله آلة

68 A Ukrainian, but now Paris-based, group of female activists, founded in 2008, who stage topless protests against the sexual exploitation of women, religion and patriarchy, among other issues. [*Trans.*]

Beyond Economic and Geopolitical Interests: The Drives

1 Qur'an 8:17 [translation adapted].

2 Qur'an 55:27.

Art, Myth, Religion

1 Qur'an 26:224–5.

Poetry Between Language and Precept

1 Badr Shākir al-Sayyāb: poet; born in Basra in 1926, died in 1964.

2 Nizār Qabbānni: Syrian poet and diplomat; born in Damascus in 1923, died in 1998. Salāh Abdel Ṣabour: poet, dramatist and essayist; born in Egypt in 1931, died in 1981.

3 Ounsi el-Hajj: Lebanese poet; born in 1937, died in 2014. Mohamed al-Maghout: Syrian poet; born in Salamiyah in 1934, died in Damascus in 2006.

4 Al-Ḥutay'a: poet born before the advent of Islam. He converted to Islam in the era of Abū Bakr.

5 François Villon: French poet; born in 1431, thought to have died c.1463. [*Trans.*]

6 Tarafa ibn al-'Abd: pre-Islamic poet. Known as 'the young murder victim', because he was dismembered and buried at the age of twenty-six. Probably died in 564.

7 *Lalangue* is a neologism (from the definite article *la* and *langue* [language]), coined by the psychoanalyst Jacques Lacan. It describes a primary, chaotic, pre-semantic (or polysemic) substrate over which ordered language is constructed. [*Trans.*]

8 From *mot*, the French for 'word', hence 'word-ology'. [*Trans.*]

9 The family of Muhammad.

10 Tayyib Salih, *Mawsim al-hijra ilā ash-shamāl* (Beirut: Dār al-'Awdat, 1969).

11 Abdekébir Khatibi, *La Mémoire tatouée* (Paris: Denoël, 1971).

How to Conclude?

1   From Friedrich Nietzsche, *Thus Spoke Zarathustra*. [*Trans.*]
2   From the poem 'Temps de vivre' ('Time to Live') by Boris Vian (1920–59). [*Trans.*]
3   Abdul Rahman Munif, *Riḥlatu ḍaw'* (Lebanon, 2008).